GOLDEN TOES

GOLDEN

ST. MARTIN'S PRESS
NEW YORK

TOES

Football's Greatest Kickers

DON KOWET

Contents

GOLDEN TOES

FROM SKULLS TO PIGSKINS

Most scholars agree that the roots of soccer, rugby and football sprouted around nine hundred years ago, in an England ruled by William the Conqueror. Beginning in 835 A.D., waves of Danish barbarians voyaged across the treacherous North Sea to sack the coastal towns of the British Isles. For the next few hundred years, these Vikings disrupted English town and country life completely, and it wasn't until after the death of Canute the Dane that William the Conqueror—crowned as king in 1066—was able to keep them at bay.

After the climactic defeat of his Viking enemies, historians tell us, William permitted his troops a seven-day furlough. As soon as they had tippled enough to feel no pain, they staggered off to the local cemeteries, where their tormentors, the Danes, had been buried. Using their swords as spades, they dug at some of the older graves, stopping when they turned up skeletons. Cursing their vanquished enemies, they began kicking skulls around—and football was born.

For years after, the "skull game" persisted in this grisly form. There were no rules and no niceties; the aim of the game was to see who could kick a skull from one town or village to another in the shortest amount of time.

Someone must have gotten tired of smashing bone with bone, for within a century or so inflated cow bladders replaced the skulls. By now the game was played in every part of the British Isles. Teams were selected from rival towns or villages. Starting at midpoint on a road between the two towns, the teams of competitors would try to move the "ball" by kicking it into the town square of their opponents. Everything short of outright murder was permissible. The game became so popular that it threatened to become a mania. Fields went untended, and cattle were left to forage for themselves. At the peak of this frenzy, "futballe" was banned by King Henry II, and until the sixteenth century anyone who dared to play futballe ran the risk of having his head placed on the executioner's block (which, of course, was the number-one spectator sport of the period.)

Eventually, though, James I rescinded the ban; in 1633 the Church of England gave its stamp of approval, and the way was paved for such future stars as British soccer's Georgie Best, on one continent, and Joe Namath on another.

The formal permission to resume the game, however, laid down certain guidelines. Instead of disrupting rural life by their random rampages across fields and trunk roads, the players were now restricted to the use of specifically designated fields. Instead of kicking the ball into the main square of the opponent's hometown, points were awarded when the ball was kicked over a goal line.

At this point, kicking was the *only* factor in football, and, in fact, the game most resembled modern soccer. (Only in the United States is the game called soccer; throughout most of the world, including England, the common word for soccer is still "football.") Several hundred years passed without any significant changes being made, until goal posts were eventually introduced, along with limitations as to the numbers of players who could participate at any one time. First called "association football" (still the official designation in Britain), the name was eventually shortened to "assoc", and finally "soccer."

Up to 1823, kicking was the entire game. But during that year a soccer game was played at Rugby College, England, that was destined to change the course of sports history. A plaque hanging at Rugby tells the entire story:

> This stone commemorates the exploit of William Webb Ellis, who, with a fine disregard for the rules of football as played in his time, first took the ball in his arms and ran with it, thus originating the distinctive feature of the Rugby game. A.D., 1823.

Not until 1846 did the school's athletic administrators actually legalize for official games the daring innovation of William Webb Ellis, and by that time the ball had come to resemble more the prolate spheroid in use today than a

3

standard soccer ball. But it wasn't until twenty-three years after the founding of the modern game of rugby that Americans got a glimpse of it. On November 6, 1869, in New Brunswick, New Jersey, Rutgers and Princeton played the first rugby match ever in the United States.

Soon soccer had infiltrated every level of the educational system, from grade school up through university. And in 1862 the first organized football club—independent of any educational institution—was formed—the Oneida Football Club of Boston.

In 1870, three soccer-style football games were played among eastern universities. First Rutgers beat Columbia, then Rutgers was defeated twice by Princeton. However, the local bluebloods were so dismayed by the bloody savagery with which the game was played (soccer, even now, is considered a working-class sport in England, while rugby is associated with the aristocracy, an association deriving from its roots in the universities). Football's brutality offended the self-appointed guardians of public morality—and football was banned in Boston (among other cities) in 1871. The ban was lifted the following year when Yale and then Stevens Tech joined the eastern league. In 1873 football clubs were formed at the City College of New York and the Virginia Military Institute.

A crossroads was reached in 1873, when Rutgers, Columbia, Princeton and Yale decided to get together to standardize the local ground rules of their brand of soccer. They had also invited Harvard to their council, but the Crimson had refused. Harvard, like Yale and Princeton, had been playing soccer since the turn of the century, but with one difference—it had become the nation's only rugby school. It was Harvard that would provide the game we know today as football.

Instead of lining up with its local rivals to play soccer, Harvard in 1874 crossed the northern border in search of rugby competition. In that year, the Crimson (whose nickname derived from the blood that flowed in their brand of rugby) scheduled two successive encounters with McGill University in Montreal. The first game was played under Harvard's rules, and the Crimson won easily. Playing the second game under Canadian rugby rules, the Crimson still managed a scoreless tie. In a third encounter later that same year, McGill won a decisive victory.

Those three games generated an amazing amount of interest in the United States. The next year, 1875, when Harvard challenged Yale to a game of Crimson-brand rugby, Yale accepted—and the traditional rivalry began.

Harvard beat Yale in that first match, 4-0, but the Elis were so entranced by this new version of football, so enthralled by its classic potentialities for mayhem, that they joined Harvard in forming the American Inter-collegiate Football Association, along with Columbia and Princeton.

At this point, the game still resembled rugby rather than the football we know today. Although the team that scored most touchdowns was the winner, a field goal (any kick over the crossbar) was equivalent to four touchdowns. Thus the art of kicking was still held supreme.

Within the next decade two important rules changes were instituted. First, teams were limited on field to eleven men each, with each man assigned a specific position. Second, the scrimmage line was written into the rules. Up to then, the rugby "scrum" had been—along with the pass in from out-of-bounds—the standard method of putting the ball in play once teams had kicked off.

In the "scrum," both sides form competing phalanxes, each man tied to his teammate by locked arms. The "scrum half" flips the ball under the legs of his teammates, who then kick the ball behind them till it squirts out into play. Meanwhile, of course—and before the ball is actually in play—both teams try to shove each other downfield. Thus it's possible to gain, say, twenty yards without the ball ever having left that tangle of churning feet.

The introduction of the scrimmage gave a streamlined look to the game. A team could kick off from the scrimmage line. As in modern-day rugby, the kick might be a towering drive downfield or a nibbler topped with the heel of the foot back to the "quarterback" behind the scrimmage line. In sum, reducing the confusion of the scrum led to a game in which tactical plays could be executed, each strategy dependent on the situation at hand.

The next rule change was the introduction in 1882 of a series of downs—which carried the idea of the scrimmage to the next logical step. Each team was allowed three downs to gain five yards. If, however, a team managed to lose ten yards before using up its three downs, the ball went over to its opponents.

The emphasis on kicking over running or passing still prevailed. A field goal was now worth five points, a touchdown merely one point. But by 1890, a touchdown had come to be valued at two points. In 1910 the field goal slipped in value to three points, while two years later the touchdown was set at a definitive six points.

Walter Camp, who rightly deserves the title of "father of modern football," initiated many of the basic rule changes that transformed the game in the late 1800's from a species of Americanized rugby into a unique sport. Camp emphasized the strategic benefits of a strong kicking game, having learned the value of punting from stars of his era—kickers like Frank Butterworth of Yale and Knowlton Ames of Princeton.

Kicking even in those days, of course, had most of the elements found in modern punting and placekicking, but with some odd—from our point of view—differences. The center passed the ball back from an upright position, with his back to the opposing linemen. Or he might face his opponents and nudge the ball back with the heel of his foot. But before the kicker could pick up the ball, it had to be touched by the quarterback—the descendant of the rugby scrum half.

Protective equipment was minimal; although the kicker effectively had a center and a conveyor-belt quarterback one step away from a holder, what he lacked above all in those days was some kind of protection from the onslaughts of charging linemen. He got no help from the referees, either. Roughing-the-kicker penalties would have struck players of that day as absurd. After all, that's what the game was all about—roughing your opponent in every way possible, with ethics conditioned by the principle that "might makes right."

One of the best of the early kickers was the University of Chicago's three-time All-American Walter Eckersall. Twice Eckersall kicked five field goals in a single game, and his punt against Michigan in 1905 led to a safety that broke Michigan's fifty-six-game winning streak.

But all previous kickers paled into insignificance when Jim Thorpe came on the scene.

2

JIM THORPE

Most of yesterday's stars wouldn't even get a chance today to prove whether they could make a modern National Football League club; in most cases, the computers modern clubs depend on for scouting advice would blackball them without a hearing as too light, too small or too slow.

Except for kickers. In line with a trend toward specialization in all of our sports today, our place-kickers and punters are sometimes men who would have been considered too puny to play by yesterday's standards—men like the dolphins' soccer-style super-kicker, Garo Yepremian. Furthermore, in kicking we can measure today's heroes against yesterday's, since the art of kicking has *always* been a strictly solo activity.

Thus, in a roundabout way, we come to the greatest

athlete this nation has ever produced, Jim Thorpe. For although we cannot measure how effective Thorpe's legendary running ability would be against today's monster linemen, how productive his bat would be against major-league pitching, or whether he could compete with our super-trackmen, what is indisputable is that Thorpe was one of the greatest kickers of this or any era.

Thorpe, a Sac and Fox Indian from Prague, Oklahoma, was an All-American football player under Pop Warner at the Carlisle, Pennsylvania, Indian School. Thorpe went on to become Olympic decathlon and pentathlon champion in 1912, a professional football star with the Canton Bulldogs, and a professional baseball player with the Giants, Reds and Braves. None of his feats were more prodigious, though, than those he accomplished with his foot. Just how great he was is illustrated by his performance against Harvard University in 1911. Harvard had gone unbeaten in 1910 to win the national championship. The entire team was back intact for the 1911 season and was three-deep at every position. In comparison, coach Pop Warner's Carlisle team consisted of only sixteen men. And Jim Thorpe was hobbled by layers of bandages taped to both legs, the result of injuries incurred in earlier games. The offensive tactic of Carlisle's opponents was always: get Thorpe. The opposition that previous week had literally tried to wrench his legs out of their sockets.

Percy Haughton, Harvard's legendary coach, sensing a mismatch between his powerful and deep unit and the skinny Indian kids from Pennsylvania, started the game with his second team, who promptly moved down the field for a touchdown (then worth five points), adding the conversion to take a 6-0 lead.

Then Thorpe began his demonstration of how effectively a kicking game could be used to offset the opponent's physical advantages. He kicked a 23-yard field goal. He kicked a 43-yard field goal. He kicked a 37-yard field goal, and Carlisle led at the half, 9-7.

But Harvard came back in the early moments of the second half to score a touchdown, then add a field goal of their own, making the score 15-9, Harvard.

"Gimme that ball," Thorpe told his quarterback Gus Welch. And Bell did, handing Thorpe the ball on nine successive plays. The Harvard line knew Thorpe was going to charge at them. Jim spun, slashed, dived and simply battered every obstacle out of his way, driving 70 solo yards for a touchdown. Then Thorpe kicked the game-tying extra point.

As the closing minutes of the game approached, it was obvious that Harvard was willing to settle for a tie. So were the Indians, for whom, as underdogs, the tie would be construed as a moral victory. Neither team could move the ball in the continuous drizzle that had turned the field into a downpour. But Thorpe refused to submit.

With the Indians on Harvard's 43-yard line and only minutes of game time remaining, Thorpe ordered quarterback Welch: "Set the ball up, I'm gonna kick it."

"But you've already kicked three," the quarterback told him incredulously.

"Then I'll just have to make it four," Thorpe replied.

A hush descended over Harvard Stadium as it became obvious to the fans that Thorpe was going to attempt an unprecedented 50-yard field goal. He stood behind his holder, his mud-spattered uniform with the bandages hanging in disarray around his legs giving him the appearance of a soldier slogging through some disastrous battle. But there was nothing defeatist about his approach to the ball, as he took his steps, then lifted his leg through an arc of pain to send the pigskin spiraling up and up and over the uprights.

After a moment of stunned silence, the partisan crowd errupted with ecstatic cheers. Their team had been beaten, but Thorpe's performance had transcended local loyalties.

Later in his career while playing pro ball for the Canton Bulldogs Thorpe kicked a 75-yarder against Indianapolis. And despite technical improvements in field construction, kicking shoes, specializations of kicking techniques, no one since has equaled that distance. And though the most dramatic of his kicking abilities, field goals were not Thorpe's only kicking talent. He was a fine punter, regularly lofting 70-yarders. When he was later asked what his longest punt ever was, he replied: "Ninety yards. It was when I was with the Canton Bulldogs. I forget," he added with characteristic nonchalance, "who the other team was."

SAMMY BAUGH

Overall, Sammy Baugh played football for thirty years. From 1937-52, he played for Washington, his sixteen years of NFL services the third highest total ever. Before his career had finished, the fabulous Texan had thrown 3016 passes in the NFL and completed 1709 of them, for a total distance of 22, 085 yards—more than 12.5 miles. And 187 of them were good for touchdowns. At the same time, he was—in those days of two-way football—the premier defender *against* the pass in the NFL. But few people are aware that Sammy Baugh was perhaps the greatest punter the game has ever known.

Over twenty years have passed since Baugh played his last professional contest, yet most of his punting records are still intact. Here are some of those records:

1. From 1940-43, Sammy led the league four times,

the most seasons leading the league in NFL history.

2. On November 5, 1939, in a game that pitted Washington against Philadelphia, Baugh punted fourteen times, a feat unsurpassed up to the present.

3. Based on the official qualifying minimum of 300 punts, Baugh's lifetime average of 44.93 yards per punt is the best ever in the National Football League.

4. His 51.3 yards-per-punt average in 1940 is the NFL record.

5. Based on a qualifying minimum of four punts, against Detroit on October 27, 1940, Baugh set an NFL record that still stands of 59.4 yards on average per punt.

Samuel Adrian Baugh was born in Temple, Texas, on March 17, 1914. He was not a "cowpoke," although for publicity reasons the fans were led to believe that he was. In fact, his father worked for the railroad, and Sammy grew up with the small town preoccupations of every American kid in 1914: sports. As a youngster, Sammy found throwing and catching balls almost as easy as walking. He was good at basketball, even better at baseball. But the sport he loved the most—and considered himself most proficient at—was football.

In high school, Baugh started out as an end, but when the coaches saw how he could rifle the ball, he was quickly switched to tailback in the single- and double-wing formations that were standard at the time. High school was in Sweetwater, Texas, where Baugh and his family had moved when Sammy was sixteen. It was there that the legendary exploits began to take shape.

In his backyard Sammy hung an old tire by a rope to the branch of a tree. Day in, day out, he would rush home from school to throw the ball through the tire. Gradually he increased the distance of his throw to the target. And when he became proficient at throwing the ball from long and short distances through the tire, he began swinging the tire before he dropped back to throw. When he was able to hit the bull's eye regularly from any distance, with the tire in motion or at rest, he added running, dodging—every other trick he could think of to simulate a game situation.

But he practiced hard in baseball, too. He could hit, he could field—and, of course, throw. When Leo "Dutch" Meyer spotted him playing on the sandlots, he recommended that Baugh be given a scholarship to Texas Christian University, where Meyer was head freshman baseball and football coach. Although Meyer had seen him play both sports, he was convinced that Baugh's true talents lay in baseball, so Sammy went to TCU in 1933 on a baseball scholarship.

Ironically, when Francis Schmidt, athletic director at TCU, got a look at Baugh's skinny (6'3", 170-pound) frame, he was sure Sammy would never make a football player—at least not in the tough Southwest Conference. Meyer, however, got Baugh to come out for the team, and was impressed with Sammy's passing ability. But, moaned the coach, that's *all* Baugh could do, and in two-way football passing alone wasn't enough. So Baugh started practicing again, this time concentrating on a talent he had up to now only used sparingly his ability to kick a football.

By Baugh's sophomore year, the Southwest had succumbed to mania for razzle-dazzle wide-open football, whose elements were essentially focused on the go-for-broke pass, buttressed by the surprise quick kick. And Baugh by now was master of both.

His meteoric college career culminated in the final game of his senior year, when he passed and kicked heavily favored Santa Clara out of the stadium for a stunning 9-0 upset. Rewarded with a trip to the Cotton Bowl, Baugh used his arm and foot to lead TCU to a 16-6 victory over Marquette, reputed to be the best team in the powerful Midwest. Baugh was All-American and expected an invitation to play in the college All-star game—which he intended to refuse. For his aim was still a career in major-league baseball.

But then he was drafted by the Washington Redskins of the NFL who gave him the highest rookie bonus ever. With Baugh, the Redskins finished second in the Eastern Division in 1938 and 1939. But in 1940 they won the title with Baugh setting dozens of passing and punting records, using the kick to surprise his opponents and set them back in poor field position. That year, in fact, he got off an 85-yard punt that was to stand as the NFL's longest for years to come.

The Redskins did poorly in 1941, but not Baugh. Again he accumulated punting and passing records. And in 1942 the Redskins regained their form, winning ten of eleven games to take the Eastern Division title. Their opponents in the championship game were the Chicago Bears, who had won all eleven of their games, while averaging 33 points per contest. And for added spice, the encounter would pit two of the best quarterbacks of all time against one another—Baugh versus the Bears' Sid Luckman. They were both great quarterbacks, runners, strategists and passers. But Sammy Baugh had one advantage over Luckman. He could kick and Luckman couldn't.

Through the first period it was a kicking game, with the edge going to Baugh. In the second period the Redskins fumbled. Bear tackle Lee Artoe gathered the loose ball in, and rambled for a touchdown, giving the Bears a 6-0 lead. The Bears missed the extra point.

Then the Bears kicked off, tackling the Redskin receiver on his own 12-yard line. The Bears and everyone in the stadium outside the Redskin huddle expected Baugh to go right to his passing game. So when Baugh took the ball and drifted back with his throwing arm cocked, the Bears fanned out laterally in a one-to-one pass defense. But at the last possible moment, Baugh lowered the ball, brought up his foot and punted far over the heads of the Bear defenders, with the ball bouncing forward, then finally downed on the Bears' five-yard line. Luckman tried a pass. It was intercepted. Baugh threw for a touchdown, and the conversion made the score 7-6, Redskins.

In the second half the Bears again anticipated a passing game from Baugh. So Sammy ran twelve consecutive plays into the middle of the Bears' line. On the last of that twelve-play sequence, Andy Farkas slipped into the end zone to give Washington a 14-6 lead.

From then on, Baugh relied on the punt to keep the Bears completely off balance. Whenever Baugh got the ball in poor field position, he simply ran enough plays to get the Bears off guard, then quick-kicked when they were least expecting it. For the Bears, it was a nightmare. It was a typical Baugh effort, and evidence of why he found himself at the end of that season the league's top punter for the third consecutive year.

But Baugh did more than just set records. He brought the punt alive as a devastating defensive-offensive weapon. He paved the way for the specialists in today's NFL who earn their living by dropping a ball onto their feet, then kicking it for tactical advantage. While the field goal can win a game for you, the punt can keep your opponent from winning it.

4

THE 1920'S AND 1930'S: KICKING DECLINES

Although Thorpe and Baugh were extraordinary kickers, there is little doubt that as the run and pass came more into prominence, kicking receded into the background. The legalization of the forward pass allowed an offensive team to gobble up significant chunks of yardage almost instantaneously. The run not only had the opposite effect of eating up the clock and giving an adept team ball control; it also provided those squirming breakaway flights of halfbacks, whose dazzling spurts captivated a nation that was becoming, in the age of the automobile and the airplane, increasingly obsessed with speed in every aspect of its life.

Still, there were expert practitioners of the kicking art during the 1920's and 1930's. George Gipp of Notre Dame was a punter who could manage 62 yards on a good day, and whose average punt sailed consistently around the 60-yard mark. The Gipper was also an expert at field-goal kicking, in the era when kickers dropped the ball to the ground (dropkick) before slamming it over the crossbar. Joel Hunt of Texas A & M was a versatile offensive threat cut from the Thorpe-Baugh mold. Besides running like a maddened bull, Hunt could execute any facet of the kicking game. On the coaching side of the game, head coach Harry Kipke guided his Michigan team through an unbeaten season in 1932 by making sure they adhered to his credo of "a punt, a pass and a prayer."

Nevertheless, kicking was on the decline, despite the individual talents that blossomed during that era. In 1934, changes were made in the shape of the ball to permit passers to throw it with less difficulty. At its thickest point, the ball was scaled down an inch; the tips, furthermore, were compressed to finer points. In general, the ball was narrowed to a more aerodynamically efficient shape.

The positive effect, of course, was a ball that a quarterback could toss for distance, with speed and accuracy. The negative effect was that the rule change effectively made the dropkick obsolescent almost overnight.

Permitting the ball to bounce off the ground on either of those newly honed-down tips was to give oneself over to the mysterious workings of chance. Dropkickers simply didn't know how the ball would react—and found the art they had struggled to master suddenly archaic.

Dropkickers in those days frequently got off boots of over 60 yards. But suddenly the kick became a major risk.

No one could control consistently the slimmed-down ball. Kickers in general found it hard to hit the ball for distances they had been accustomed to achieving, because this smaller ball was both harder and heavier than previous models.

The pros, of course, had their kickers, too. The American Professional Football Association had been organized in September of 1920. Two years later, it became the National Football League. One of the best of their early kickers was Paddy Driscoll. Against Columbus in 1925, he drop-kicked four goals,—18-, 23-, 25-, and 50-yarders. The next year Elbert Bloodgood of Kansas City also managed to send four field goals past the up-rights via dropkicks. But the big name from the late thirties onward belonged to "Automatic" Jack Manders who led the NFL in field goals in 1934, 1936 and 1937. In 1934 and 1937, in a preview of kickers to come, he actually led the NFL in total points scored.

Punters, too, scattered some foot-bound glory into the record books during that era. Wilbur Henry blasted one against Akron in 1923 that was tape-measured at 94 yards. Ken Strong and Sammy Baugh, of course, counted kicking among their multitude of talents.

But it was not until the advent of kicking's first pro superstar in the 1940's that the art of hitting the ball with a foot regained the eminence it still held in rugby and soccer. Singlehandedly, that man was to initiate a trend that is still developing today—that of the kicking specialist, the clutch performer who enters the game only in crucial situations to kick for offensive or defensive advantage; the point-scorer, the executioner.

His name was Lou Groza.

5

LOU GROZA

The emergence of Groza as an NFL superstar marked the dawn of a new era in professional football. For the first time, the kicking specialist received the recognition (and salary) traditionally accorded to the glamour positions of the game—the running backs and quarterbacks.

Groza had prepped for his eventual starring role with the Cleveland Browns at high school in Martins Ferry, Pennsylvania. Martins Ferry is a rugged factory town 60 miles from Pittsburgh. The Grozas (including Lou's younger brother Alex, who would also star in NFL football until he was implicated in a gambling scandal) were a big sprawling Hungarian family. Lou's father was a towering man who owned a pool hall in which he himself served as bouncer. At the end of Prohibition, "Big Spot," as he was known, converted the pool hall into a bar and restaurant. By the time they were in high school, any day "Big Spot" found trouble he couldn't handle alone, his boys were big enough to provide assistance.

Lou, although he eventually grew to a 6'3", 240 pounds, was the smallest, his eldest brother Frank the biggest. Frank was the placekicker for the Martin's Ferry High School team. The summer before he performed for the varsity, he convinced his younger brother to practice with him seven days a week.

After Frank graduated, Lou took his place at the placekicking tee, between boots manning a tackle slot. Brother Frank became his coach. There were telephone wires strung above one end of Mill Field, and for want of a better goal post, these served. In his freshman year, Lou was a better tackle than placekicker—until the final game of the season, when for the first time he demonstrated the clutch potential that would bring him NFL fame. Against Blair, Martin's Ferry's traditional rival, Lou kicked a late-in-the-game 35-yard field goal for a 15-14 victory. By the time he was a sophomore, Lou was an accomplished kicker.

From the beginning, he was a perfectionist. Besides practicing hour after hour after regular practice, Groza developed two rules of procedure that were to count heavily toward developing his effective technique. First, from high school on he developed the habit of focusing his eyes on the ball at the moment of impact, which forced him to keep his head down from the start of his approach to the ball until it was in the air. Second, he reminded himself constantly to kick the ball with his toe up in order to get the proper lift into his kicks.

From high school, Groza (having become an All-Ohio tackle) followed his brother Frank to Ohio State. In the middle of his freshman year he was called to active military service and was not released until the war ended in 1946.

In the interim, he had come under the gaze of Paul Brown, who had been following Groza's career since Martin's Ferry. When Lou entered the army and was stationed at Fort Sam Houston in Texas, Brown sent him friendly letters. When Groza was transferred overseas to Leyte in the Pacific, Brown kept corresponding—and not just for the sake of friendship. Already germinating in Brown's mind was the vision of a new professional football franchise in Cleveland. He intended to build a dynasty, and had the foresight to see that a super placekicker was an essential cornerstone.

After Groza was released from the army, instead of buying a ticket back to Ohio State, he headed for Bowling Green and the new Cleveland franchise's first training camp.

That Brown had his kicking cornerstone was evident in his first regular game in the All-American Conference, against the Miami Hurricanes. Lou Groza contributed three field goals and five extra points, as the Browns won 44-0.

"Anywhere inside the 50," Brown was soon telling reporters, "we never have to punt. We just let Lou go for the field goal."

Tactics like that enabled Groza to appear often enough to kick 45 extra points and 11 field goals during that '46 season, as the Browns won their conference championship.

In fact, though, in the early days of the old conference "The Toe" was usually called on to kick for field goals from between the 30-40 yard marks at maximum. And then one day the Browns got stuck just beyond midfield. Paul Brown was about to follow the usual practice of the time and send in his punter, when he noticed Groza warming up along the sideline.

Why not gamble? he asked himself.

"Hey, Lou," he called over. "You can't kick one that far, can you?"

Groza measured the distance with his eyes, then turned to his coach. "Who says I can't?" he replied.

Brown sent Groza into the game, and in a precedent-setting moment, Groza kicked a 49-yard field goal. From then on Brown's dogma of Groza-at-the-fifty-yard-line became a reality. Thus, Brown was able to exert a new kind of pressure on his opponents. Groza's ability to kick the long ball consistently, and Brown's willingness to use it as part of his standard coaching tactics, put pressure on an opposing defense from up to 50 yards in front of their goal posts. It was a radical departure in offensive football. Even the 50-yard line had to be considered a danger zone.

More and more Brown came to rely on Groza's toe to make the decisive difference in a game. Eleven times Groza kicked three field goals in a single game, with the Browns winning nine of those encounters. And in the two losses, Groza scored all the points.

However, after the 1949 season, the All-American conference folded. The best teams in the league were absorbed into the National Football League. Everyone predicted that the All-American conference teams would be patsies for even the worst teams on the NFL.

But Paul Brown's team believed in themselves, not the press. With Otto Graham passing to Mac Speedie and Dante Lavelli, with Marion Motley blasting past linemen like a bulldozer, and with Groza consistently sending the football between the uprights, the Browns decimated the NFL's Eastern division, taking the title by beating the New York Giants, 8-3, with Groza kicking two field goals.

The 1950 title playoff matched the Browns against the Los Angeles Rams. Beside the money and the title, there was an element of local pride at stake. The Los Angeles team had originally begun as the Cleveland Rams; some years back they had deserted Cleveland, and now, with a new team, the Browns, the fans were demanding vengeance.

That Sunday in December was a blustery, raw winter afternoon, with a biting wind stinging the faces of the 30,000 spectators, and sub-freezing temperatures turning the playing field into yards of concrete. Bob Waterfield was the Rams' quarterback, Otto Graham was Cleveland's. The game was a seesaw encounter in which two great offensive teams played up to potential.

With two minutes of game time remaining, and the score 28-27 in favor of the Rams, Waterfield dropped back to punt. The Browns' Cliff Lewis caught the ball and ran the kick back to the Browns' 32-yard line, stepping out of bounds to stop the clock.

There were fifty seconds left in the game.

With Paul Brown calling the plays and quarterback Graham executing them to perfection, the Browns moved downfield to the Rams' 16-yard line.

There were twenty seconds remaining.

Now every spectator knew what Brown's next call would be. Everything would depend on the specialized skills of Lou Groza, who had trotted nonchalantly out on the field and was carefully marking the spot from which he would attempt the crucial field goal.

A few minutes before, a mischievous gust of wind had torn the ball away from Groza's holder, spoiling the chance for an earlier field goal. So now Lou checked and rechecked the wind direction—it was strong, and blowing the wrong way.

30,000 fans were silent.

The center passed the ball back, the holder jammed its tip into the ground, while Groza took his steps and kicked. The ball rose against the wind, went up and over the crossbar for the game-winning points.

When the final gun sounded, Lou's teammates grabbed him and lofted him onto their shoulders. And although the fans and players were unaware of it at the time, Groza's importance that day was a hint of the future—when in the 1970's, placekickers would almost dominate the game.

6

BETWEEN GROZA AND GOGOLAK

The Groza era brought back to football something old—the ancient preeminence of kicking; something new—the carping of critics who began to claim that kicking was getting too much prominence in modern scoring; something borrowed—the soccer-style field goal and punt, dating from the advent of the Gogolaks; and something blue—Alex Karras and his cohorts, who insisted, against all reason, that kickers weren't authentic athletes.

Critics began making suggestions for rules changes as early as the late 1950's, and haven't stopped yet. Kicking, the critics ventured, had become too easy—the field goal too effortless a way to score three points, the point-after-touchdown too automatic. But the rules makers weren't listening. In 1958, the rules committee of the American Football Association eliminated the automatic point-after-touchdown attempt. Instead, it offered the team scoring a touchdown the option of kicking for one point, or running or passing for two points.

In 1959, the rules committee shook up their book again. In that year—in a move that could only affect placekickers—they shifted the width of the goal posts from 18 feet, 6 inches to 23 feet, 4 inches.

Thus, the AFL had done exactly what the critics had not wanted them to do. While taking the staleness out of the automatic extra point, they had also widened the goal posts, tempting more coaches to try for field goals in tight situations. Since that date, in fact, there have been more field goals kicked every single year, at high school, college and professional levels.

In 1966, seven of the top scorers in the AFL and in the NFL were kickers; in 1971, the top seven scorers in the NFC and the top ten scorers in the AFC were all kickers. And there is never a lack of candidates at any level of competition. Every year professional tryout camps are overrun with men of all heights, ages, physiques, degrees of talent and education, all of whom have only one common denominator: They think they can kick in the National Football League.

"Garo Yepremians," Eagles' personnel man Herman Bell calls them. "People see this little bald-headed guy from Cyprus in a football uniform and he's sort of an inspiration. So, they start writing you letters asking for a tryout."

In fact, though, as we shall see later, kicking is—along with quarterback—perhaps the position in football that demands from a player the most exacting technique coupled with a commensurate ability to withstand terrifying pressure.

The final trend, of course, is that which we see unfolding before us. It began with Pete Gogolak, who was signed by the Buffalo Bills as a free agent in 1964. The second soccer-style kicker to crack the pros was also a Gogolak—Pete's younger brother Charlie. Charlie set his precedent when, after finishing his varsity football career at Princeton, he became the first draft selection of the Washington Redskins—the first pure kicker ever to be chosen first by an NFL team. Then came Jan Stenerud, Bobby Howfield of Denver and the New York Giants, Toni Fritsch of the Dallas Cowboys and other kickers.

Simultaneous with them, of course, the conventional kickers still figured among the top scorers in both pro conferences. Jim O'Brien of the Baltimore Colts, ageless Lou Michaels of Green Bay, Fred Cox of Minnesota, Jim Turner of the Jets, Errol Knight of the Redskins, Eric Mann of the Lions, Bruce Gossett of the 49ers and the rest.

Meanwhile, tiny Hillsdale College in Michigan was producing a soccer-style kicker of Polish descent named Chester Marcol, and before Marcol was drafted into the pros for the 1972 season, experts were already predicting greatness for him. The Dallas Cowboys had given him a 4.8 grade on their five-point scale.

"He is the best placekicker and punter I have seen this season," said no less an authority than Lou Groza in 1971. Among Marcol's accomplishments in 1971 was a 62-yard field goal—only a yard under Tom Dempsey's NFL record.

And some experts have already prophesied that our

conventional kickers will be replaced totally by European soccer-style kickers, perhaps within the next three years.

"I think the soccer style permits you to kick farther," says Pete Gogolak. "For accuracy, straight ahead is just as good. Our way we can put much more power into the ball. Think of the swinging motion of hitting a golf ball. You put your body into it. But the straight-on kicker seems to punch the ball with his foot."

After the soccer-style kickers entered the game, there were scads of time and motion studies devised to test the best way of kicking a ball. The results were inconclusive.

Sports Illustrated once sponsored an overseas contest in which two Americans, Sam Baker and Mike Mercer, faced some of the best kickers of rugby and soccer in Britain. Mercer won, but the British complained (and rightfully so) that the test really proved nothing, given the British unfamiliarity with the ball and similar factors.

Says Bob Kap, special scout for the New Orleans Saints (Tom Dempsey's ex-team): "American kickers are for the birds. They have no future and are inferior to soccer-style kickers in technique and accuracy. Pointing to the example of former Austrian soccer hero Toni Fritsch, who successfully converted to the American game after signing with Dallas in 1971, Kap adds:

"Fritsch is far better than Dallas' conventional kicker, Mike Clark."

That's perhaps true, although only time will tell if Fritsch wins his duel with Clark. However, is Yepremian better than Cox, is Stenerud better than Turner? Off the statistics, Gossett, for example, has been having more success than either of the Gogolaks in recent years, and

Michaels has scored more points than any active kicker. Finally, few will dispute that the best kicker of all was a conventional kicker, Lou Groza of the Cleveland Browns.

The soccer-style partisan could retort, with some justification, that the best kickers in the world—the Bobby Charltons of England, the Peles of Brazil, the Georgie Bests of Ireland, the Bechenbauers of Germany—are soccer players.

But it's one of those strictly partisan arguments that only time can answer. As far as we are concerned, a young kicker should learn the style available to him from the coaches at hand. It does not matter which style he adopts, the mechanics are fundamentally the same—the self-discipline and mental toughness is equal. The basic advantage that European kickers have, in our opinion, is not their soccer-style technique, but the fact that from the time they are old enough to walk, there is a ball constantly at their feet. We do not believe there is any inherent advantage in the soccer-style kick. We contend that soccer-style kickers owe their recent success in American football to the fact that all they have done, all their lives, is concentrate on kicking. It is our belief that if two boys of equal talent begin to concentrate on kicking at the same age, with equal coaching and equal motivation they will arrive at the same level of proficiency. The style is irrelevant. What is important is to begin to learn how to kick *today,* and to concentrate on kicking until you master it.

Says Jan Stenerud: "Kicking is more natural to Europeans. Give a European boy a ball and his first instinct is to kick it, not to throw it. If a European starts kicking an American football, he'll probably be better than an American who has never done it before. I can't help but think there must be someone, somewhere, maybe in Asia, who can kick the football even better than me, because I never thought about kicking a football until I tried. The first time I kicked one, I kicked it almost as well as I'm doing now."

Needless to say, of course, Stenerud is being modest. Every kicker must improve. The kicker who stops learning is the kicker who is *unlearning* what he has previously internalized.

Pick your style, experiment till you find the one that suits you. Style, you see, doesn't really count in sports. The chain can be red or blue or orange; no matter what the color, its strength depends on how well each individual link is built.

The step-by-step mechanics are the links in your kicking chain. Master them.

7

THE GOGOLAKS

Strangely enough, the abortive Hungarian revolution against the Russians eventually catalyzed a revolution in American football. For with the attendant displacement of persons, the refugees streaming away from the zone of armed conflict, history repeated itself. The original Anglo-Saxon settlers of America had carried their game of rounders with them to their new homeland, and the game eventually grew into baseball. Rugby transported 4,000 miles across the sea was transformed into football. And a Hungarian refugee, a Budapest physician named Dr. John E. Gogolak, transported—in the form of his two young sons—the germ of a new (for Americans) kicking technique that threatened years later to make conventional techniques obsolete.

The amazing thing, of course, is that Americans were

able to endure so long without discovering the soccer-style placekicking and punting techniques. Soccer is the game that attracts the largest number of spectators in the world by far. It is the game in which a man's legs are his livelihood, his arms merely a balancing pole. Of course, we were aware of the kicking prowess of soccer stars—Pele is a household name even in the United States. But two factors kept coaches from trying to adopt the soccer-style kick: the fact that kicking itself only recently became a crucial part of the game and the belief that soccer styles would work only with the round soccer ball.

The Gogolak brothers helped dispel both illusions.

Arriving in the U.S. at the age of twelve, Pete Gogolak and his brother Charlie (three years younger) had grown up with a soccer ball constantly snuggling up to their shoes. Pete was in high school at Ogdensburg, New York, for a full year before he realized that football also involved kicking. "I hadn't heard anything about football when we came here," Pete recalls. "And I didn't try out for it until some friend said to me that I was big enough to go out for the team." Pete soon proved to his coaches he had the size (6'2", 205 pounds) and the toughness to play American football, and made the varsity in his first attempt, as an end. Then, the Friday night before the first game of the season, the coach told his squad he needed kickers and asked for volunteers.

Pete was one of six who agreed to try out. After three of his teammates had kicked, Pete's turn came. As is customary for soccer players—and second nature to any boy growing up in a soccer-playing country—Pete stood at a 45-degree angle to the ball's intended line of flight.

"One kid said, 'Why don't you try to kick the ball toward the goal post?' " Pete says. "I was kicking a soccer ball that way since I was four. I thought why should I do it differently. When I kicked it, it was good, but it was a line drive, too low. They all stood and looked. They'd never seen it before."

His coach was mystified. But no intelligent coach argues with success, so Gogolak became Ogdensburg's kicker. The only coaching anyone felt capable of giving Pete was on how to get more loft into his kicks. How he kicked, the coaches agreed, was his business.

Pete graduated from Ogdensburg into the Ivy League, and the cries of "Go Go Gogolak" became a victory anthem for Cornell.

And the same refrain was soon being heard from the Princeton rooting sections. Charlie Gogolak had also gone the Ivy League route, and was having success equal to his elder brother's.

When Pete graduated from Cornell it was with ambitions to try his soccer-style technique in pro football. But NFL scouts in general, locked into their own traditions, looked on him as some kind of freak. "I got calls from the Vikings, Eagles and Colts," Pete says, "but nobody picked me in the NFL draft. Actually I was not well known in football, but I knew I could play. I was prepared to pack a bag and to go to tryout camps, but then the Bills finally offered me a job."

And what a job Pete did for the Bills! In his first year, 1964, he was second to the Patriots' Gino Cappelletti in field goals. In 1965, he led the league. Later Pete went to the New York Giants, where he currently handles placekicking chores.

While Pete was opening the eyes of pro-football fans to the soccer-style kick, Charlie was creating his own kind of glamour waves at Princeton. Starting from a 70-degree angle (as opposed to Pete's 45-degree angle), Charlie was proving that the soccer-style kick was a technique worth imitating. Devastating opponents with field goals up to and past 50 yards in distance, Charlie caused most consternation at Pete's alma mater, Cornell. In the 1965 Princeton-Cornell encounter, Cornell coach Tom Harp devised an unorthodox defense to counter Charlie Godolak's unorthodox kicking style. Harp's field-goal defense consisted of putting two backs on the shoulders of mammoth linemen in hopes of deflecting any low trajectory kicks.

Charlie watched the construction of this human pyramid with amazement. Then he stepped up and arched the ball for a 54-yard three-pointer.

"I was amazed when I saw the pyramid formation," he recalls. "I thought the defenders were horsing around. I would have liked to have hit one of those top guys in the head," he added with a grin.

Charlie, who at 5'10", 165 pounds is a frailer-looking version of his brother, claims that standard soccer techniques give the soccer-style kicker control and coordination unknown to native-born Americans. "When I was a kid," he says, "and right up into the pros, I used to practice every day balancing a soccer ball with my foot in the air for at least ten minutes, without it ever touching the ground."

This—and all the other techniques second nature to kids

who grow up with a ball on their foot as naturally as American kids grow up with balls in their hands—led Charlie after graduation to the National Football League and the Washington Redskins.

8

GEORGE BLANDA

When George Blanda had his super year in 1970, leading Oakland to its division title and winning for himself the Most Valuable Player award, there was a tendency among fans and sportswriters alike to view his saga in the light of "life begins at forty." But the idea that Blanda suddenly sprang to prominence after an obscure career with a bevy of teams is way off base. For while Blanda did give hope to the geriatric set, his performance in 1970 was merely a ripple in the even flow of a super career.

As a matter of fact, up to that 1970 season George Blanda owned or shared 37 individual professional football records. Among them: He had scored more points than any player in the history of the game; he had played more games; he had scored in more consecutive games; he'd led the league in points-after more often than any other player; he'd thrown more passes in a single game; he'd completed more passes in a single game. Along with Y.A. Tittle, he'd thrown more passes in a single season; along with Adrian Burk and Joe Kapp and Y.A. Tittle and Sid Luckman, Blanda had thrown seven touchdown passes in a single game. He owned field-goal records and AFL records and conference championship records . . .

More relevant to Blanda's status as a placekicker, although the media made fans throughout the nation aware of Bert Rechichar's "longest field goal ever" record the day New Orleans' Tom Dempsey broke it, very few of us knew that George Blanda had been runnerup to Rechichar with a kick only one yard less—a 55-yarder in December, 1961. A year later, in fact, Blanda kicked one for 54 yards. And while through the years most of us naturally thought of Lou Groza as the most prolific goal kicker of all time, the fact is that through 1969-70, Blanda had kicked 240 field goals to Groza's 234. By the end of 1971, in fact, Blanda had kicked an amazing total of 271 field goals and 780 extra points over his 20-year career.

In part, of course, we tended to gloss over Blanda's achievements simply because there were so many of them. The fact that he is one of the best quarterbacks of all time tends to overshadow his ability as a kicker. The process works in reverse, also, muddying our image of him. His career has been so long, with so many zeniths, that two generations of football fans have had to learn separately what kind of magic Blanda can perform on a football field.

Blanda grew up in the Pennsylvania mining country that has developed so many future football stars. Like Lou Groza, Blanda was descended from East European (Czech) immigrants. Like Groza, he imbibed the tough miners' philosophy with his bottled milk: Be independent, know how to fight, and endure. With periodic mine shutdowns, early on Blanda, his six brothers, and his four sisters, knew poverty and the struggle for survival. "We competed for everything," he recalls. "Even the food on our table."

So football was a way out, the only viable foothold in the steep climb toward material prosperity. That meant a scholarship to the University of Kentucky, where Blanda submitted to the tough discipline of coach Bear Bryant, as relentless a taskmaster as any mine foreman.

At 6'2", 180 pounds, Blanda was used early on as a blocking back and punter. But in his junior year, Bryant converted him to quarterback and set his style for the next two decades. Operating out of the T-formation, Blanda became a pinpoint passer, a short-range missile-launcher expert at throwing the low bullet pass off a quick release.

When Blanda graduated from Kentucky in 1949, he signed with the Chicago Bears. And thus began a long love-hate relationship between Blanda and the Bears' dictatorial owner, George Halas.

His first year, Blanda was third-string quarterback behind Sid Luckman and Johnny Lujack. Overshadowed by the two eventual Hall of Famers, Blanda was primarily used as a placekicker. Determined to stick with the pros, he perfected his kicking technique to the point where the Bears could not afford to dump their third-string quarterback. From 1949 on, he kicked 156 consecutive points-after-touchdown before finally missing one in 1956.

In the interim, of course, Halas and he were conducting a war of nerves. Halas, one of the founders of professional football, had little use for kickers. Having grown up in the blood-and-guts eras of Thorpe, Grange and Nagurski, Halas had no use at all for "specialists," with their particular needs, their unique equipment. Halas refused to buy Blanda a specialized kicking shoe, so Blanda bought his own. According to Blanda, Halas refused to let him practice kicking field goals for longer than two or three minutes a day.

Halas' attitude toward kickers in general and Blanda in particular was summed up in a rare piece of Halas humor. In the 1956 title game, with the Giants ahead 35-7 and little game time remaining, Halas turned to Blanda and said: "Go in and beat 'em, kid."

The Giants won, 47-7.

In 1960, Blanda escaped the grasp of Halas and signed with Houston of the newly formed American Football League. And suddenly, after having spent eleven years in relative obscurity with the Bears, he became a star at thirty-three. Three years in a row Blanda quarterbacked the Oilers to the AFL title final, winning two of those games. Then, in the middle sixties, came a decline in the number of his completions and an alarming increase in the number of times his passes were being intercepted. So in 1966, with Blanda now thirty-nine, Houston put him on waivers, and Oakland signed him for a pittance.

Blanda began at Oakland in even worse position than he had begun with Chicago. Now he was No. 4 quarterback, behind Daryle Lamonica, Cotton Davidson and Charlie Green.

But he could kick, and again his foot saved him from oblivion. "Let's face it," he once said, "my foot has kept me in this game."

From 1966 to 1969, Blanda did more than endure. Gradually he moved up to backup quarterback, filling in admirably whenever Lamonica was unable to lead the club. In 1969, though, when coach Madden played an injured Lamonica instead of going with George, Blanda popped off—and a few days before his forty-third birthday, found himself on waivers again.

But Blanda was, in a sense, saved by his—for football standards—advanced age. No one wanted him, so General Manager Al Davis decided to keep him on as insurance behind Lamonica. But it still looked like the end of his career. In the second game of the 1970 season, against San Diego and with a tie score, Blanda missed a game-winning field-goal attempt from the 32-yard line. "Blanda the kicker is probably fading away," said one writer. "He appears unsteady at the field goal line, like Ben Hogan hanging over a putt."

And then the unexpected occurred. At forty-four, Blanda turned into an authentic phenomenon. On October 25, against Pittsburgh, he replaced a crippled Lamonica and tossed three touchdown passes in the fourth quarter for a spectacular 34-14 victory. The next week, against Kansas City, Blanda entered the game with the Raiders behind by three points and with eight seconds left in the game. With the Chiefs' 6'9" Morris Stroud positioned under the goal posts, Blanda attempted a 48-yard field goal. When Blanda kicked, Stroud leaped high into the air, but the ball sailed inches above his outstretched hands, giving the Raiders a tie with no game time remaining.

Against Cleveland that next Sunday, Blanda threw a

pass with twenty-five seconds left to bring the Raiders into the Browns' territory. Then, with three seconds on the game clock, and the score tied at 20-20, Blanda booted a game-winning 52-yard field goal. The following week he beat Denver with a touchdown pass in the closing minutes. Against San Diego the next Sunday, Blanda came into the game with sixteen seconds on the clock and kicked a field goal that won the game for Oakland, 20-17. Later Oakland beat the Jets, 14-13, with Blanda quarterbacking, then kicking the PAT for the winning margin.

Blanda went on to an equally successful, if less dramatic, season in 1971, kicking 41 extra points and 15 out of 22 field goal attempts for 86 total points. But both the irony of his sudden leap to stardom and the tremendous importance that kicking had come to play in the modern pro game, did not escape him.

"Winning these awards makes me chuckle a little," he said after being awarded his MVP trophy. "I threw 36 touchdown passes in one season and kicked 456 extra points in the American Football League, and that was nothing. But now I kick a couple of field goals and all of a sudden I'm a star."

9

FRED COX

The Cleveland Browns' 1962 preseason training camp in Hiram, Ohio: It was a fairy tale out of the old West, the fastest foot in the NFL taking on the challenge of an upstart from the University of Pittsburgh. So every day, after the Browns' regular drill, coaches and players would huddle along the Main Street sideline to watch the head-to-head duel between Lou Groza, veteran of sixteen pro campaigns, and young Fred Cox. Today's drill was the dress rehearsal for the season's opener against Detroit the following Sunday.

Cox kicked first, after coach Fritz Heisler had paced off 37 yards, then set the ball down on its nose. Cox proceeded to kick seven of ten attempts for field goals. After the rookie had finished, the legendary "Toe" Groza approached the 37-yard marker with the studied nonchalance of a man with countless clutch victories to his credit. Effortlessly, he matched the rookie's seven for ten.

Then the football was moved back about 10 yards. This time Groza hit three for five, while his challenger managed to convert only two.

Groza held his advantage throughout the next "event"–kickoff practice, and finished the day with a slight advantage.

Afterwards, coach Heisler said: "Fred is by far the best rookie placekicker we've had since Lou came along in that first 1946 season. Most of the others became quickly deflated when the Toe powered a few."

Nevertheless, it was youth versus experience, Cox's ability to hit for distance against Groza's phenomenal accuracy. The end result could have been assessed a draw, but the old boxing adage held: You have to *beat* the champion to take over his title; a draw is as good as a loss.

A few days after that final competition, Fred Cox was cut from the Browns' roster.

Of course, that Cox had even been able to compete with Groza and remain competitive throughout training camp was a proof of how much pure potential he had. For until his senior year in college, Cox had kicked fewer than five field goals. The first time he had ever kicked in a game situation was as a sophomore in high school, a less than promising debut. Cox hit the ball and it dribbled about 12 yards downfield until one of his teammates recovered it. It was, needless to say, one of the most abortive field-goal attempts anywhere at any time.

"To this day, people in my home town think I did that on purpose," Cox says. "I was the most surprised person on the field and so were my teammates, but I never let on that it was an accident. And I don't know how many times since then I've tried to duplicate that kick, but I just can't."

In fact, had he depended on his kicking, Cox would probably never have reached the Browns' training camp in the first place. Throughout high school, he'd been a 5'10", 200-pound power back, and had led his Pennsylvania high school team in rushing statistics. On scholarship to the University of Pittsburgh, Cox was his team's leading rusher for three consecutive seasons. He was drafted by the Cleveland Browns. Shortly after he injured his back.

"I wouldn't be kicking if it wouldn't have been for my back," Fred says. "I was drafted as a halfback. But I was hit on the hip and it drove my back out of place."

Two strands of Cox's future destiny were spun out of this fateful injury. On the one hand, Cox developed a deep and abiding interest in chiropractic, eventually becoming a chiropractor himself. On the other, his part-time experience as a punter and placekicker suddenly turned into his only means of livelihood. In effect, then, the competition between Groza and Cox produced no losers. For although Groza booted Cox out of camp, he landed right on the turf of the Minnesota Vikings.

And again the element of luck, according to Cox, played a crucial role in the turn his career took for the better. "In 1963 [the year after his tryout with Cleveland], when the Vikings brought me back up, Mike Eischied was also trying out," Cox recalls. "But because I had been up the year before, the Vikings let me kick in the first exhibition game. I kicked five field goals and Mike never got to kick at all."

That first year with the Vikings Cox did the punting, too, averaging a respectable 39 yards per kick. But Cox convinced coach Bud Grant that his punting chores were hurting his placekicking, so the Vikings relieved him of the punting in 1964.

"You can't do both successfully," Cox argues. "If you kick well one day, you usually punt poorly, or vice versa. The Vikings thought so much of my punting ability that they lost no time drafting a punter the next year."

Characteristic of the man's modesty, the field-goal attempt Cox remembers best from his rookie year was one that failed. Against Green Bay, Cox trotted out on the field for what should have been a game-winning field goal. "But I missed it," he says, "and to add insult to injury, Green Bay ran it back for a touchdown."

It was a rare miss. From 1963 on, Cox's trademark became his consistency. Along the way, he managed to set some records, scoring in 122 contests and kicking field goals in 29 straight games, including an amazing 25-yard effort into a 40-mile-an-hour wind one Sunday in 1970 against Green Bay.

"The wind was so bad," says Cox, "that all four flags were blowing in different directions."

He also holds club records for scoring, the number of field goals and the longest field goal—a 53-yarder in 1965. The last time he missed kicking an extra point was the season's opener in 1968. In 1970, Cox was awarded the Viking team's Most Valuable Player award, after scoring 112 points, only two below the NFL's best. In 1971, Cox's 91 points were fourth best in the NFC, but he ranked

50

second in number of field goals made (23). And his .687 completion ratio was the best in his nine-year career.

Overall, Cox ranks second to Green Bay's Lou Michaels among the NFC's top ten scorers. (Michaels, of course, has the advantage of having played in the NFL thirteen seasons, four more than Cox). However, Cox ranks first among active players in number of field goals completed (188).

Cox, of course, is constantly ribbed by his teammates about the lack of contact he endures as a placekicker. In 1969, for example, against the Chicago Bears, when he attempted a field goal, a Bear lineman dove through and blocked the kick, with the ball bouncing back into Fred's hands. Cox rammed his way up field for a key first down. When he came off the field, a Viking coach remarked that his uniform "had to be sent to the laundry for the first time this year."

But, Cox says, he can live without the contact. "I used to miss running at first," he says, "but now whenever I think about running, I go over to the cooler and get a drink of water."

10

JIM TURNER

Nineteen sixty-eight was the year of the New York Jets and Joe Namath. "And we're going to win next Sunday—I'll guarantee you," became Namath's prophetic equivalent to Babe Ruth pointing his finger at the Yankee Stadium bleachers before he hit that legendary home run. Speaking in Miami, Namath guaranteed that his team would win the third Super Bowl, thus making what had previously seemed a routine NFL victory into something special—a chance to see Namath crushed. But the Jets did the crushing, 16-7 in the biggest sports upset ever.

But Namath hadn't done it alone. That season Jim Turner kicked field goals at a .739 pace, setting a season's record of 34 field goals and 43 extra points for 145 total points—an all-time pro record for a pure kicker. Entering the 1972 season, after eight years in the AFL and NFL,

Turner ranked second among active scorers to George Blanda (whose point total, of course, includes nine touchdowns). Currently, Turner's totals are 256 extra points plus 178 field goals for 790 total points. In 1971, Turner was fourth in AFC scoring with 93 points, including 18 extra points and 25 field goals out of 38 attempts. Overall, he's the AFC's tenth-ranked all-time scorer.

From high school on, of course, it was obvious that Turner would excel at some aspect of athletics. The question was where. He grew up in Crockett, California, a town located on the headwaters of San Francisco Bay. "Crockett isn't one of your precious little pastel California Dreamin' kinds of towns," Turner says. "It's the real world, with about 4,000 real people in it. It's a hell of a little town, and everything there is great. You can let your little girl walk across town to go to kindergarten. When you can do that, you know you're in a pretty good American town."

As a kid, though, Turner found Crockett constricting. But now he's the town's celebrity. "They put up goal posts for me when I'm in town," he says. "So that I can practice kicking. They even gave me a key to the locker room and unlimited use of the whirlpool bath," he adds with a chuckle.

The locker room and whirlpool are located at Swett High School (enrollment 550), Turner's high school alma mater. At Swett, Turner was a star in two sports. In his senior year he captained and quarterbacked the Swett Indians to an undefeated football season. He also starred in swimming.

54

"It wasn't swimming like you have today," he says, "with that age-group stuff that encourages little girls to swim faster than I ever did as a strong young man. I swam the freestyle sprints and the individual medley, turned the 100-free in about 55 flat. Back then, swimming was part of something bigger called water sports, which included skin diving and water polo and water skiing and surfing. I mean, if you loved the water you did everything in it."

From Swett High, Turner went to Utah State, where he played quarterback on the same team with future pro stars Bill Munson, Merlin Olsen and Lionel Aldridge. Turner graduated from Utah State in 1964 into the Jets' training camp.

Starting with the Jets in 1964, he set numerous league and conference records, a number of which still stand. In 1969 he attempted 47 field goals, a conference record; in 1968 and 1969 he converted 34 field goals, a league record. From July 1966 through November 1967, Turner kicked field goals in 18 consecutive games. Naturally, he holds almost every conceivable Jet club record for kicking.

But although Turner has seen service almost strictly as a kicker, his high school and college grounding as a quarterback has led him into the Jets back field in practices and even a game or two. But, inevitably, he's justified his paycheck with his foot.

A typical Turner day was the one in 1969, against the Cincinnati Bengals. On the first offensive sequence, the Jets moved 44 yards to the Cincinnati 26 and gained 4 more yards on two runs and an incompletion. Time for Turner to kick a 23-yard field goal.

The second time the Jets had the ball, they advanced 24

yards to the Cincinnati 34. Emerson Boozer lost three yards, a completion to tight end Pete Lammons gained three yards and Namath underthrew a pass. Time for Turner's 41-yard field goal and a 6-0 lead.

The third time the Jet offense got hold of the ball they drove from their 29 to the Bengals' 42. Matt Snell was stopped at the line of scrimmage for no gain on the next play, with Namath then throwing two successive incompletions. So they called out Jim Turner again, and asked him to kick the second 50-yard field goal of his pro career.

He did.

Having proved himself an essential part of the Jets' offense, Turner bridles at the suggestion that placekickers aren't really football players.

"These people who ask me if I feel like I'm part of the game give me a pain," he says. "How can a guy not feel that way when he produces so many points? Just because a guy doesn't go out and get hit every play doesn't mean he's not a player. I spend a lot more time on the field than a lot of our substitutes," he adds. "Should they be called players and a kicker not? I say no!"

Again we come back to the crucial differences not only between kicker and the rest of his teammates, but say, lineman and quarterback. For there are similarities between what it takes, mentally, to play quarterback and placekicker. The kicker enters with no real warmup, for one play, often with the game on the line. His position is equivalent to the professional pinch-hitter in baseball—or would be if a pinch-hitter were expected to hit a home run *every* time he bats. Only the quarterback experiences those momentous situations when the fate of the team depends on his arm, when only the long desperate bomb will snatch victory out of the jaws of the defeat. But, if the play is bungled, the quarterback can always lay some of the blame on his pass defense, a poorly run route by his receivers; for him, win or lose, any single play will be viewed in the overall context of an entire game.

But the field-goal kicker—if his holder places the ball properly—must accomplish his task by himself. He cannot blame the wind, for he is expected to compensate for it, understand it. He cannot blame the ground conditions, for he is expected to anticipate them. And if the game is close, a failure to convert will not be easily forgotten, since he may have the chance to win the game by himself, he also can—in the eyes of fans, press and even his teammates—lose it by himself. In sum, at his worst moments he is an easy scapegoat.

Fortunately for the Jets, Jim Turner has endured few of those moments. Turner was subsequently traded to the Denver Broncos for soccer-style kicker Bobby Howfield.

11

JAN STENERUD

By a strange coincidence, there's a memorial to Knute Rockne not far from Fetsund, Norway, where Jan Stenerud was born and raised. Decades ago Rockne had left the mountain town of Voss to travel to South Bend, Indiana, where he created the legend of the Gipper and Notre Dame's most glorious football era. As a child, Jan Stenerud recalls having seen the memorial to Rockne once. It was in English, and young Jan didn't understand English. He didn't understand American football, either. Like most Europeans, football seemed to him a muddled, overcomplicated and senseless barbarism—rugby in armor, a throwback to the times when metal-plated knights clanked their way across bloody European battlefields.

True to the tradition of his nation, what *did* interest Jan, and what he *did* understand, was skiing. In fact, the only reason he was aware of the Rockne memorial at all was because it was on the route to Holmen Kollen, the world's highest ski jump, where 100,000 people attend the most prestigious sports event in Norway.

But although he knew little of Rockne, Stenerud was later—in the game that had made his countryman's name a household word in the United States—called upon to demonstrate the kind of courage in the face of adversity that Rockne had made legendary.

A top skier in Norway, after the Norwegian equivalent to high school, Jan was recruited by Montana State College on a four-year skiing scholarship. En route to Montana, he stopped off in Buffalo, New York, where Larry Felser, a local journalist, took him out to see the Buffalo Bills play at War Memorial Stadium. It was the first time Stenerud had ever seen the game that had won Rockne that '(to Norwegians) incomprehensible plaque in the village of Voss.

"What impressed you the most?" Felser asked him after the game.

"The noise," replied the kid from the quiet mountain village. I never heard so much noise."

Years later, when he missed a crucial kick that put his Kansas City Chiefs team out of running for the Super Bowl, the noise in Stenerud's ears would be intolerable and haunting.

At Montana State, Stenerud won three NCAA ski-jumping titles. He also met his future wife, Lani, who in turn introduced him to college football. Jan still understood nothing about the game and cared less, but one day, while he was running laps around the football field in preparation for the upcoming ski season, he joined some friends who were kicking on the practice field. His soccer style and his tremendous distance and accuracy impressed Montana State's football coaches to the point where they first convinced the skiing team, then Stenerud, that the best interests of all would be served by converting Jan's skiing scholarship to a football grant.

In his senior year, Stenerud started for the Montana varsity. When he kicked a 59-yard field goal against arch-rival University of Montana, the noise that erupted from the stadium full of fans echoed all the way to Kansas City, who drafted him the next year and made him their starting placekicker.

His first season in the league, Stenerud had tremendous success, scoring an NFL rookie high of 108 points. His total dropped his second year, due to a groin pull suffered in preseason exhibition game. In 1969 and 1970, however, he was back in the groove. And in 1971 he scored 110 points, including 32 extra points and 26 field goals out of 44 attempts.

But that 1971 season was marred by one significant failure. Stenerud's career was stained by having failed to turn one of those transitional moments where an athlete can become hero or bum to his favor.

By December 25, 1971, Jan Stenerud had become the third highest scorer in the American Football Conference. In only five years in the league, he had managed to kick 180 extra points and 134 field goals, many of them under extreme pressure. But from Christmas day on, until the start of a next season and the opportunity for vindication, the only kick Jan Stenerud could remember was the one he missed. And wherever he went he was reminded of it. Just a couple of weeks before, Stenerud's 10-yarder in the final minute had killed Oakland's Super Bowl chances, 16-14, and the week before that he had gotten off a 54-yarder against San Francisco. Those two games had climaxed Stenerud's late season rush, helping to convert his worst season into one that would have been respectable for most other placekickers. Against Buffalo, he had kicked five field goals, four against the San Francisco 49ers and three against the Raiders.

"I had some trouble early in the year," Jan recalls. "I had some blocked and I hit the goal post a couple of times. But I felt I came along pretty well and got in a nice groove—until the last one."

Over and over he relived—before the start of the 1972 season—the 31-yard field goal that he missed, three points that would have given the Chiefs a victory over the Miami Dolphins in regulation time—eliminating the necessity for playing what was to become the longest game in NFL history. In his dreams he carries an engraving of a football sailing toward the goal post, then veering outside the uprights by inches.

This is the indelible image: center Bobby Bell scoops the ball back to holder Len Dawson. Stenerud takes his roundabout soccer-style approach to the ball, seeing it lift off his foot, on line for the uprights, but with just fractionally too much altitude. Then curving, curving, mischievously away from the goal posts . . .

Ed Podolak had carried the ball to the 31-yard line on the previous play. "When Podolak made his run I got up and started to get loose," Stenerud recalls. "I felt nervous and a little tense, but I always do before I go in to kick. When I got in there I felt there was no way in the world I could miss. I thought I hit the ball reasonably well, but I got under it. The field may have been a little rough," he adds. "You're always looking for a high spot.

"On Sunday I didn't think I'd watch the Miami-Baltimore game, but finally I did. After seeing Miami handle Baltimore, I began thinking that we could have won and the misery started all over again."

Despite the fact that in only five seasons with the pros Stenerud has scored 582 points, he will never, he realizes, escape the stigma of that single crucial miss. "What the hell do they know about football?" Alex Karras once asked of placekickers.

Stenerud can answer: The pressure, the frustration, the timelessness of a moment in which a career is at a crossroads and behind the convex face mask and the awesomely accurate kicking leg is a man, with a wife, young children, hobbies, an off-season job as a bank president. At least the folks back home in Fetsund were unaware of his darkest moment.

The first time Jan brought films to his parents in Norway to show them how he earns his living, his father said: "I see you getting up and I see you sitting down, but what do you do the rest of the time?"

Strange echoes of Alex Karras.

12

TOM DEMPSEY

It was November 8, 1970, and there were forty-five seconds left in the game, with the Detroit Lions leading the New Orleans Saints, 17-16. The ball was set on the Saints' 37-yard line, when to the amazement of almost everyone in the stadium, the Saints' chunky 6'1", 265-pound placekicker, Tom Dempsey, lumbered onto the field to attempt a record 63-yard field goal. To most, Dempsey's presence on the field was a tacit admission of defeat by the Saints. After all, the NFL record was 56 yards. No one would break the record by seven yards.

Of course, players were aware that the 60-yard hit had been routine on many NFL practice fields for years. But no one had come even close to achieving it under the pressure of a game situation.

"I've kicked them 60 yards in practice," Dempsey

recalls. "This time I had the wind at my back. My main idea was to not only hit it square, but in addition keep it in line.

"Joe Scarpati—a great holder—was set up a yard deeper than usual, at 8 rather than 7 yards. I don't usually tell the fellows anything before I try a field goal," Dempsey adds, "but I went into the huddle and said, 'Fellows, this is going to be a pretty long one—so give me an extra second of blocking.' "

It was enough. Dempsey stepped up at the snap from center and kicked the longest field goal ever. Ironically, Alex Karras, the great blood-and-guts lineman who had taunted Yepremian in particular and placekickers in general throughout his years with the Lions was among the vanquished who watched their victory flying away along the trajectory of Dempsey's kick.

That Dempsey ever made the pros, of course, is an achievement, a triumph of self-discipline and courage, which overshadows what he accomplished on any particular Sunday. From birth Dempsey has had only half a foot on his right leg and no right hand at all. Ironically, fans throughout the country only became aware of his disabilities when a New Orleans paper tried to correct them in a photograph. It was 1969, and a newspaper ran a picture of Dempsey kicking the crucial 19-yard field goal that gave the Saints a last-gasp victory over the Giants in New York. The paper's artist, unaware of Dempsey's birth defects, saw the stub Tom was kicking with and assumed it was a defective photo, the result of faulty transmission on the wire. So he grabbed his brush and quickly restored Dempsey's missing foot.

66

In fact, throughout Dempsey's career people had refused to accept the fact that he could even function in sports. Some of them were surprised he hadn't given up on life the day he was born. Neighborhood kids in his native Encilitas, California, a small resort town on the Pacific shore just north of San Diego, called him "Stumpy" and "Captain Knob" and other names even more cruel.

"Kids are basically cruel," Tom says, "but in a way that was good for me. The nastier they got, the harder I worked to overcome the problem."

And his parents encouraged him not to consider himself handicapped. "I learned as a kid from my father that there was no such word as 'can't.' He'd make me try everything, and I wouldn't be satisfied until I was good at everything I tried. And in high school my coach wouldn't let me feel different. I had a tendency to feel sorry for myself. When you're a kid," he adds, "every kid wonders: Why me? But the only real reaction I had to it was a challenge. People would say I couldn't do something, and I just don't believe the word can't exists."

Sports—which depend to a large extent on native physical abilities—was the arena in which Dempsey decided to prove that he was as good as the best. "I was an All-Star first baseman in the Little League," he says. "In high school and college I threw the shot—in college over 50 feet."

He started out in high school as a tackle, wearing a shoe that had been sawed in half and sewn. Sometimes he'd hear an opponent say, "Aw, this guy can't do nothin'."

"I'd go out there and knock the hell out of him," says Dempsey.

From high school, he went on to Palomar Junior College where he became an all-conference end. He started kicking in his second year. Still wearing that sawed-off shoe, he placed tape across the front foot stub. At the end of that second year, he quit school and signed with the Green Bay Packers. But the pact was declared invalid because Dempsey's class hadn't graduated yet, so the Packers sent him to play with their farm team in Lowell, Massachusetts.

When he wasn't playing he was wrestling in local arenas for money. But the real money was in the future, dependent on what that half-foot could do on a football field. He gained renown in the Atlantic Coast Football League that year by kicking a 57-yard field goal. The next year, 1968, he returned to San Diego and signed with the Chargers.

But a rookie from SMU, Dennis Partee, beat him out for the starting placekicker's job, and Dempsey spent the entire year on the taxi squad. After that season of frustration, Dempsey asked for—and obtained—his release from the Chargers and turned up at the San Diego training camp of the Saints. Soon Charley Durkee, the Saints' starter till then, was on the bench, with Dempsey handling the placekicking chores. His 55-yarder against the Los Angeles Rams was but a preview of things to come.

Then came 1970 and the 63-yard kick. It should have been that last lunge upward that carries an athlete over the precipice onto a plateau of acceptance. But it wasn't. After the 1970 season, the Saints changed coaches. And that decision catalyzed the corresponding change in Tom Dempsey's career.

J.D. Roberts, who replaced Tom Fears as head coach before the 1970-71 season opened, was a tough ex-marine, ex-pro star who believed in streamlining the mind of all thoughts except football and streamlining the body of every ounce of excess fat. The first thing Roberts did when Tom reported to camp that summer was to guide the placekicker to a scale. By the time the needle had stopped climbing upward, Dempsey was considerably poorer. Roberts leveled a fine of $1 for every one of the 25 pounds the coach declared as excess fat.

It was a bad start for coach and placekicker. It was destined to get worse.

"For the first time in my life I let a man really get to me," Dempsey says. "I let my emotions, my hatred for this man get in my way and it ruined my kicking. It was my fault, I suppose," he adds. "In the pros they don't pay you to like or dislike a man. They pay you to kick a football."

Dempsey couldn't or wouldn't lose weight. After all, he argued, he'd always weighed in around 265-271. How could Roberts arbitrarily designate him overweight when he had performed miracles the previous season?

And Roberts was a Legree for discipline, calisthenics, exercise till you fell flat on your face from exhaustion. "I used to dread going to practice," Dempsey recalls. "I started worrying about the kicks I missed and everything just piled up. I knew if it continued I wouldn't be there long."

He wasn't. Roberts cut him just before the regular season opened, but what irritated Dempsey most was *how* he lost his job. "The kid he sent in, Skip Butler, kicked off three times out of bounds and made a 12-yard field goal and that's what it took to get my job," Dempsey says bitterly.

But even this unexpected reversal of fortunes couldn't damage the confidence of a kid who had already overcome the stigma of half a foot and no right hand to fight his way into the NFL record book. Dempsey joined the Philadelphia Eagles, operating under new head coach Ed Khayat. Khayat had taken over the Eagles, ruling them with an iron hand. But, like Lombardi at Green Bay, instead of alienating his players, he was able to convince them that his methods were to their mutual benefit.

Dempsey's weight did not interest him at all. As long as his placekickers got results, Khayat said, he could play at whatever weight he wanted to.

Dempsey was brought up from the Eagles' taxi squad for the Eagles tenth game of the season. In his first four games he kicked 10 of 14 field goal attempts, including a 57-yarder against the Washington Redskins. In his third game, against Detroit, he kicked a 52-yarder. The next week, against the St. Louis Cardinals, Dempsey kicked four more. Overall, after his late start in 1971, Dempsey booted 12 field goals in 17 attempts. His .706 average was best in the National Football Conference.

Ironically, his runner-up was the man who succeeded him at New Orleans, Charlie Durkee, who in a full season of play had kicked 16 of 23 for a .696 percentage.

A happy man again, Dempsey says: "I hear the cheers, I'm not going to tell you I don't. I love it. I enjoy playing football. I get a kick out of every Sunday," he adds, "and no pun intended."

70

13

GARO YEPREMIAN

In five years in the league he's made physical contact with opponents only twice. He's bald, short at 5'7", he weighs his official 172 pounds only wet and in full game dress. His wife's most common term of endearment for him is the Worm—and yet Garo Yepremian is a Super Bowl hero and full-fledged superstar. That is a measure of how far the game has moved from the days when Jim Thorpe dominated every aspect of the game on field.

Just how much Yepremian means to the Miami Dolphin offense shows in the scoring statistics. In 1971, Garo kicked 33 extra points and 28 out of 40 field goals for 117 total points, the highest total in both the National and American Football conferences. It's an unlikely event that turned a pint-sized Cypriot immigrant into the scoring king of the game dominated by ton-and-a-half offensive and defensive lines, educated from childhood to grunt their shoulders into the muscled stomachs of speedy 220-pound running backs. Even quarterbacks—the most specialized position in football until the advent of the pro placekicker—were limited by the weight-and-size syndrome. Pro clubs are constantly scouting for quarterbacks tall enough to peer over rushing linemen, meaty enough to fight off tackles and still release their bombs.

But, after Yepremian, it's doubtful that anyone will ever worry about a potential kicker's size again. In pro terminology, Garo simply doesn't have size—and yet he's the most devastating scoring machine the game has ever known.

"I hate these little feeble foreigners," Alex Karras once said, in an oblique reference to the Lions' then-placekicker Yepremian. "They get in a game for 20 seconds, win it with a field goal, then go running off the field yelling, "I keek a touchdown, I keek a touchdown.' "

Yet Yepremian endured to escape from the Lions and go to Miami. After Karras was cut, Yepremian was still scoring points. Still, the image haunted Yepremian—the image of somehow being unmanly because he was relatively small. But Yepremian shares attitudes in common with all great athletes, primarily, besides his superb kicking ability, a tough, uncompromising and indomitable attitude. When uniform numbers were distributed at Miami, he announced: "I want the number one, because I want to be the number-one kicker in football."

In 1970, he led the NFL in scoring accuracy and finished third in points scored. In 1971, kicking during one streak an incredible 16 field goals out of 19 attempts, Garo finished on top in every category. The left-footed soccer-style kicker produced the winning points on consecutive weeks in November against Pittsburgh and Baltimore. Throughout, he proved that he was deadly accurate, short or long, up to 50 yards. But most of all he proved what kicking theorists have long suggested: Size and strength are not essential prerequisites for the successful placekicker.

But determination is essential, and Yepremian has it in abundance.

He learned his English in a private school in Larnaca, Cyprus. "We were not rich," he says, "but I did everything the rich kids did. My father sold fabrics, yard goods, off a truck. My mother made shirts so my brother and I could go to private school. We did everything—we played tennis, got guitar lessons, got soccer coaching from one of the best coaches in Europe. I would wear out a soccer ball every six months."

But when Yepremian was fifteen, the good times ended. His family moved to England, and Garo went to work as a cutter in a clothing factory, then as a salesman in a men's goods shop. The customers were primarily Italians, Frenchmen and Germans—so he picked up smatterings of these languages to add to his fluency in Armenian, Greek, English and Turkish.

In 1966, just a few months after he'd arrived in the United States, Yepremian was making headlines as a placekicking sensation for the Detroit Lions, kicking six field goals in one game and four in a single quarter.

In 1967, however, the salad days ended. He was able to

kick only six field goals all season. He spent six months in the Army that year, and was cut by the Lions when he returned to Detroit. He became depressed, stuck to himself.

"I would see people in the street in my neighborhood in Detroit," he recalls, "and they would say, 'You never were any good anyhow; they kick you out, didn't they?' I couldn't say anything back to them," Garo adds, "because whatever I said, I couldn't prove it. So I just stayed away from people. I made ties [now a prospering Yepremian business] and I watched television. I spent too much time not wanting to go out where people could see me."

When he got the chance to play for Miami, he vowed he wouldn't waste this opportunity. When the 1970 season opened, Karl Kremser was Miami's kicker, but not for long. In the second game of the season, Yepremian kicked 31- and 42-yard field goals. The next week he kicked one 47 yards and on the following Sunday four more against Buffalo. From then on, he never looked back.

Of course, Yepremian's experience is not devoid of bone-crushing memories. There was that afternoon while playing for the Lions that he was introduced on field to one of the great linebackers of all time, Ray Nitschke. Herb Adderly was returning a kick, and Nitschke was blocking for him.

"Nitschke came straight at me and hit me in the face with his elbow," Garo recalls. "He knocked me back 15 yards. I felt very bad that this was happening," he adds with classic understatement. "It was my second pro game. We were losing 45-7"—and Garo was losing his teeth.

"But later in the locker room," he adds, "I heard a guy

say, 'Hey, Garo can take it pretty good.' That made me feel better. I had a bloody towel in my hand and I threw it down. Then I started walking around with blood all over me, acting like I owned the place."

In fact, though, Yepremian is a self-effacing personality, ready to tell you about his weaknesses as quickly as more star-struck athletes will recount their strengths. On Thursdays, when the Dolphins practice against the opposition offense, Yepremian plays wide receiver. "In eleven weeks last year," he says, "I caught five passes. I have no speed and no moves—other than that I am a perfect receiver."

Alex Karras didn't want him around. But somehow it's a fair guess that Garo's humility and excellence, his guts in standing up to bigger men and his "winning attitude" would have endeared him to even tougher men than Alex. Somehow, if Yepremian had been playing at Green Bay instead of Detroit, Vince Lombardi would have found a way to live with him.

14

THE ART OF PLACEKICKING

Is the kicking game really important? Kansas City Chief coach Hank Stram argues that it can decide between four to six games per season, minimum.

"By that I mean all phases of the kicking game," he adds. "If a team doesn't have a good punter and placekicker, it's in trouble. Look at the teams that have been successful through the years. They've had three things: a quarterback, good defense and the kicking game. I have seen too many fine teams, with excellent offenses and defenses, blow a game on a punt return, a blocked field goal or a weak punt."

Still, on the surface, kicking seems like the easiest aspect of football to excel at. A placekicker, as we have already heard, trots onto the field, performs his duties in perhaps a minute, apparently having done nothing more complicated than stepped toward a ball that his holder has positioned for him and kicked it at goal posts that seem, from the vantage point of the stands, an ample target.

Or the punting specialist, whose appearance in the game may be just as brief, who is not—as far as the observer is concerned—restricted by even having to *aim* for a target. Seventy yards anywhere downfield, the casual fan thinks, and he's earned his paycheck.

And yet, in fact, the kicker—precisely because he is the ultimate specialist—must possess perhaps the most finely honed technique of any player on the team. He must have the steely cool of the marksman—there are usually no second chances. All the pressure the quarterback faces throughout a game are, for the kicker, telescoped into a few single moments of intense concentration.

And the skills he brings to the game are not the product of luck, nor can they be attributed solely to "natural talent." In a sense, the kicker is the man we should find it easiest to identify with. No longer are there prerequisites of height and weight and strength. According to Garo Yepremian, "It's a strange thing, kicking. Usually, when I try to kick the ball with all of the force of my leg, the ball just doesn't go anywhere. Because it's all how *well* you kick it, not how *strong* you kick it."

Thus, while few of us have the physical size to fill the outsized shoes of a Bubba Smith or the raw native skill of a Unitas, we should be able to identify with a Yepremian or a Stenerud. Not that the kickers haven't got tremendous talents, but natural talents serve only as groundwork for kickers. More important is technique—master, through intensive training, of the innumerable factors that make the collision of toe or instep with a football result in a trajectory worth three crucial points.

PLACEKICKING

There are three types of placekicks employed for offensive advantage in football today: The field goal, the conversion after touchdown and the kickoff. A fourth technique, drop-kicking, is virtually unknown by practitioners of football below the age of 50.

In our discussion of some of the past and present kicking specialists of pro football, we've seen the importance of field-goal kicking to the overall offense of a club. It's probably worth summarizing those advantages here:

1. Successful field goals are usually the quickest way for a team to get on the scoreboard, and in these days of super defense, where ball control is the aim of every coach, time is an important factor.

2. The field goal is usually the least complicated way to gain an advantage in the score. Football at the high school, college and pro levels has increased in complexity enormously over the past two decades, with zone defenses and multi-option offenses. Middle linebackers, in fact, are becoming the defensive equivalent to quarterbacks, calling plays to offset the stratagems they anticipate from their opponents' offensive unit. With a more flexible deployment of defensive linemen, quarterbacks will come to the line of scrimmage equipped with a set of "audibles"—codes they will call out to change the predetermined play to counteract the defensive alignment in front of them. From Bump-and-run to the special

offensive maneuvers specially prepared for do-or-die situations, or the last two minutes of each half, in every way the game is becoming more and more complicated. And the risks of error increase in direct proportion to the increasing complexity.

A field goal attempt, however, reduces that complexity to manageable proportions. The ball, at the moment of the kick, is stationary between the holder's finger and the ground. Linemen are simply blocking out. No one need be concerned with downfield assignments. And the kicker's target is yards wider than the outstretched hands of even the tallest pass receiver.

Furthermore, unlike a receiver, the goal posts are stationary—the kicker is only concerned with the direction, heights and angle of his kick. He does not have to be preoccupied with the element of *timing*.

3. There is no risk of the interception, leading to improved field position or even a touchdown for the opponent. Since the field goal is generally attempted from no farther than 50 yards out—and most placekickers are capable of kicking considerably farther—there is usually no run back, with the attendant possibility for a long-gainer.

4. A field goal that misses its target, yet manages to pass out of the end zone, is automatically brought out to the 20-yard line. Here again the fact that there is usually no run back, that the coach can count on his opponent's starting the next series of downs deep in their own territory, is an important tactical consideration.

5. The field goal is also an equalizer in terms of team strengths. No matter how weak a team may be offensively, if it can manage to push past its 50-yard line (or even 40 in

some cases) and has an expert placekicker, it can and will score points.

The proof of the effectiveness of the field goal is its frequency. More and more, when inside their enemy's territory, coaches are trying for the field goal, rather than passing or running on fourth down, which was the traditional solution before the modern kickers came to prominence.

POINT-AFTER-TOUCHDOWN

Under the rulings established by the NCAA in 1958, college teams playing in member conferences have the option after a touchdown of either kicking the extra point or running or passing for two points. In professional football, since the merger of the AFL and NFL, the extra-point attempt after a touchdown has been mandatory. And while there's been a certain amount of criticism of the extra-point having become "automatic," the men who play football view it differently. Said Minnesota Viking coach Dan Devine recently, at a testimonial honoring defensive lineman Alan Page as the NFL's player of the year for 1971:

"In one game early in the season, Page stormed through to block a try for the extra point, leaving the score at 6-0 against us. We came back later to score two touchdowns and two conversions, making the score 14-6 going into the fourth quarter. And anyone who thinks 14-6 is only one point different from 14-7 just doesn't know football. 14-6, where the other team has to score at least twice to catch up, is a whole different type of ballgame."

Jim Thorpe, the first of the great kickers, gets off a punt. Note the lack of headgear and the long mudcleats on his shoes.

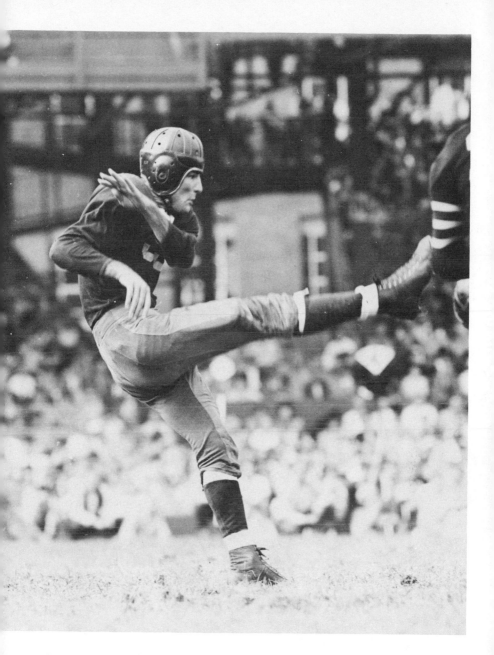

Slinging Sammy Baugh, better known for his passing exploits, was
also an adroit kicker. In this 1942 shot Baugh is kicking for the
Washington Redskins against the Chicago Bears.

Lou "The Toe" Groza breaks the mark for consecutive conversions with this 1952 PAT for the Cleveland Browns, giving him six for the afternoon and 85 in a row.

George Blanda, the ageless wonder, kicking for the Chicago Bears in 1949. Note the leather helmet without chinstrap or faceguard.

Blanda in his latest incarnation as first string kicker and second string quarterback for the Oakland Raiders. His holder is first string QB Daryle Lamonica.

86

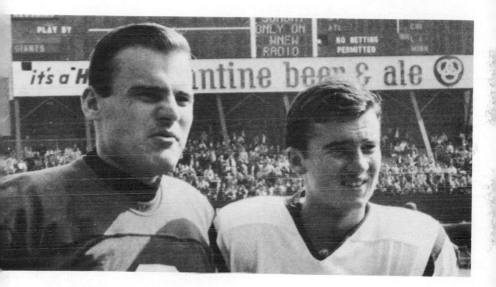

The Brothers Gogolak relax before Giants-Redskins tilt in 1966 in
which they will kick against each other.

Charlie Gogolak of the Redskins puts a 37 yard field goal through the uprights.

But Pete Gogolak of the Giants kicks two field goals and the Giants take the game 13-10.

Jan Stenerud of the Kansas City Chiefs, one of the best of the soccer style kickers, tees one up here.

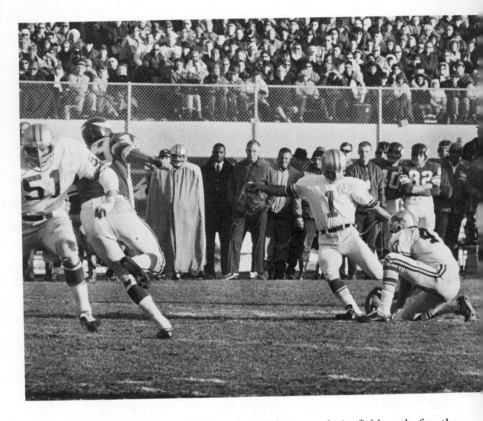

Garo Yepremian kicking one of his record six field goals for the
Detroit Lions against the Minnesota Vikings in 1966. Yepremian
now stars for the Miami Dolphins.

90

Tom Dempsey kicking his record-breaking 63-yard field goal for the
New Orleans Saints to defeat the Detroit Lions in the last second of
a 1970 contest 19-17.

Fred Cox of the Minnesota Vikings, one of the game's steadiest kickers, is a former running back turned kicker. His classic form is also displayed on the cover of GOLDEN TOES.

The extra point, then, is taken for granted—until it's missed. Thus it adds another element of excitement to a game already brimming with possibilities.

KICKOFF

The third variety of placekick in modern football is the kickoff, which follows touchdown, field goals, and safeties, and begins the game and the second half. Technique (and strategy, as we will see in the next section) count here, too—to prevent the run back, to capitalize on an opposing special team's weakness or to attempt to regain possession of the ball (the onside kick).

Let's look at the field goal and the try for an extra point first, for the mechanics of kicking each are similar. But first let's consider how the ball gets in a position to be kicked in the first place. Let's look at the role of the center and the holder—the role they play in effective placekicking.

The center, of course, must shovel an accurate pass back to the holder, and at the same time brace himself for the charge of the opposing lineman. A bad pass breaks the center-to-holder-to-placekicker rhythm so essential for an effective kick.

The holder, on the other hand, has no responsibilities except those related directly to kicking the ball. He is, in fact, an extension of the kicker—a third arm, so to speak, and he must be aware of the kicker's time sequence, style of approach and personal habits.

Likewise, the kicker must be aware of his holder's idiosyncrasies. It's not chance that the holder on professional teams is often the first- or second-string quarterback. Intelligence, spontaneity and ability to kneel firm in the shadow of towering linemen are prime prerequisites for the job. Kickers are by nature perfectionists; their success depends on doing the same things the exact same way every time they kick. Quarterbacks understand that mentality—they usually share it. They know that a fractional deviation in technique can spoil a pass or a kick.

Technically speaking, the holder is responsible for lining up the ball so that it, the center and the kicking tee (when used) are on a straight line running to the exact midpoint between goal posts. The general rule of thumb is for the kicker to set up his tee—allowed anytime in college, but only on kickoffs in the pros—approximately seven yards behind the line of scrimmage. Any closer and linebackers or a safetyman have such a short angle of rush they can sprint in and smother the kick. If the tee is set up beyond seven yards, the blocking angles of the offensive linemen become too broad, the line tends to become porous and again the chances of the kick's being blocked are high.

If the college field-goal kicker is rightfooted, the holder kneels down with his left knee opposite the tee, with the right leg directed toward the line of scrimmage. He extends his arms and hands forward, providing the center with a target and calls off an audible code to tell the rest of his teammates that the kicker is ready. He'll then gesture toward the center to indicate that he and the kicker are ready for the snap. In college and high school football, as soon as the holder has the ball he places it on the tee, holding it there with either the finger or fingers from the right hand on the very top of the ball, laces forward, the ball angled slightly toward the kicker. Experienced holders place the ball on the tee as quickly as possible, spinning it once placed to get the laces facing away from the kicker. (If the kicker hits the ball on the laces, the ball tends to curve away.) The holder holds the ball in place until the kicker boots it out from under his fingertips. The same basic procedure holds when the tee is not used.

Kickers with good sense stay on good terms with their holders.

"A holder can kill you if he wants to," says the Jets' Jim Turner. "He can give you the white knuckle—hold the ball down real hard when you get your toe into it. Or he can tilt it just half an inch one way or another. Then the whole equation goes kaboom!"

The Cards' Jim Bakken recalls the 1966 season, when in midstream he had to change holders. For the first nine games, with quarterback Charley Johnson holding, he had 15 hits in 19 field-goal tries. But then Johnson was injured and Bob DeMarco—a center—became Bakken's holder. Of his next 21 attempts, Bakken converted only 8!

Besides the human assistance provided by the center and holder, there are mechanical aids to placekicking, the use and understanding of which is crucial to a proper placement. Beside the tee, the kicker's main concern is with his special kicking shoe.

The essential ingredient of a kicking shoe—as opposed to any other type of football shoe—is the built-in kicking toe on the right foot. The sole must be made of one unbroken piece of leather, reinforced with a steel plate. Half-soles make the shoe too flexible, and for that reason kickers generally replace the entire shoe, not just a portion of it, when there's a break, or when the shoe becomes too flexible.

The NFL's supervisor of officials, Mark Duncan, periodically checks the shoes and throws out the ones with too much metal in the toe, or the ones that are double-laced.

"I've looked at some shoes," he says, "that were so heavy I could hardly lift them."

The kicking toe itself should be built into the shoe, with a surface at least 1½ inches wide. The shoe should also be a tight fit, tighter than an athlete would normally wear, to provide the kicking foot with maximum *feel*.

Now the kicker has his equipment. His center knows what is expected from him, his holder understands the crucial conveyor-belt function he plays in the successful kick. All that's left is for the kicker to approach the ball and loft a long spiral, bisecting a crossbar 40-odd yards downfield at an angle.

15

HOW TO PLACEKICK

In the normal course of his performance the kicker's primary consideration must be to follow through with the proper mechanics of getting off a successful boot. Coming in usually in a pressure-packed situation, he must, of course, be able to shrug off the tension laid on him by a stadium full of fans and the expectations of his teammates and coaches.

In taking his stance, the placekicker should line up from between two to three strides behind the spot where the holder plans to position the ball. These should be his own strides—normal, free-legged paces, the length of which will depend on you and not extraneous factors such as the length of stride of a particular NFL kicker.

But once he finds through practice the distance most comfortable for him, he should attempt to kick from that exact distance on every occasion. For, again, the standardizing of technique is important to the successful kick. The mechanical ingredients of placekicking must become second nature, pure reflex.

Most coaches recommend a stance with the kicking foot slightly ahead of the non-kicking foot, although a number of kickers do start off with their feet just about even. The idea of starting off with the kicking foot slightly in advance, of course, is to place the weight of the body on the other foot, giving impetus, like a sprinter's, when the first step off the kicking foot is taken.

The stance for the soccer kicker differs in that instead of taking his steps back and setting up directly behind the ball, he positions himself at a 45-degree angle to the ball, to the left of it if he kicks with his right foot, to the right of the holder if he kicks with his left foot. In both cases, the first step will be taken by the kicking foot.

There are, incidentally, some coaches who argue that a kicker should not artificially measure off the distance from his stance to the ball, but should simply settle for that distance which gives him the best results. Most think, however, that the two-to-three-steps-back rule is the most effective, with a kicker making minor variations in distance to accommodate his personal style.

Once the kicker has taken his stance, he drops his arms, letting them hang slack at his sides. The kicking toe should be lined up with the middle of the crossbar of the goal posts. The kicker's shoulders should also be parallel to the goal posts, with the knees bent slightly forward to give the body the proper lean into that anticipated first step.

The kicker now focuses his eyes on the spot delineated

by the holder—the spot where the holder is going to position the football. He does not focus on the center; he does not watch as the center snaps the ball to the holder. Focusing directly on the kicking spot, he can also see the holder's hands. When the holder moves his hands out, the kicker knows that the ball has been snapped. Although peripheral vision allows him to see the snap, his attention must be on what is happening to the holder's fingers at the kicking spot. The kicker begins his approach when the ball reaches the holder's hands.

Although the kicker took his stance up to three strides behind the holder's spot, the approach to the ball should require no more than a stride and a half. The kicker makes his first step with his kicking foot, which he had positioned approximately six inches ahead of the non-kicking foot when he took his stance.

This first step is a tight, short step to gather momentum. Too long a first step may throw the kicker off balance, jar his rhythm and cause him to arrive at the ball either too close or too far away.

The kicker's second step, with his non-kicking foot, is more of a lunge designed to carry him to a point approximately six inches away from the ball. If the non-kicking foot arrives closer to the ball than six inches, there will be no room for the kicking foot to get power into the boot, and the kick will be smothered. On the other hand, if the left foot is farther behind the ball than six inches (approximately), the kicker will have to reach for the ball. In all likelihood, his accuracy will suffer.

If his toe is directed upward when he kicks, he'll hit the ball high; if his toe is down at the moment of contact, the trajectory of the kick will be low and the kick will probably be batted down by the charging defensive backs who angle in across the path of flight.

Throughout, of course, the placekicker keeps his eyes glued to the very spot on the ball he's going to kick, the exact target of his toe.

So the kicker is in mid-motion, his left foot planted six inches away from the ball. Reducing this sequence to slow motion for purposes of clarity, the next frame in our kicking reel would show the kicker's total weight on that non-kicking foot, with his kicking foot beginning to move through the arc that will bring it in contact with the ball. The knee is flexed, until the moment when the pendulum swing brings foot to ball, with the toe up, the kicking heel down.

Fractionally before foot meets ball, the arc of the leg is transformed into a straight line, with the ankle and knee locked into the line of the leg. This form holds true both for conventional and soccer styles, the only difference between the two at this point being now how the leg kicks, but what part of the foot is brought into contact with the ball. (The toe in conventional kicking, the instep in soccer-style.)

In both styles, the toe is up, heel down. In soccer style, the instep is brought into contact with the ball, so that the foot, instead of pointing downfield, is until the moment of contact pointed along the 45-degree angle of approach. But with contact, the leg arcs toward the direction of kick, with the kicker pivoting slightly off his non-kicking foot into the direction of kick.

But the kicking mechanics aren't over when the kicker

100

makes contact. As in pitching, passing or hitting the batted ball, follow-through is just as important for the successful kick as what preceded it.

First and foremost, despite those spectacular photos sports editors love to fill their Sunday supplements with, at no time during the kick should the kicker's non-kicking foot leave the ground. While coaches may dispute whether all or a part of the non-kicking foot should retain contact, the consensus is that to leave the ground is to run the risk of losing one's balance, making the kick deviate because the tension of the kicker's body is directed more toward keeping himself upright than toward the proper follow-through with his kicking foot.

Also, when the kicker does leave the ground, his toes tend to curl, giving the ball an end-over-end flight instead of the aerodynamically appropriate spiral.

What the kicker *should* do, however, is get up on his toes with that non-kicking foot, to provide maximum force for his kick. Bending the knee of that leg is also advised, to keep the kicker's weight from urging him forward and past the kicking spot.

But whatever motion the kicker adapts best to—soccer style or conventional, with the non-kicking foot flat at contact, or up on the toes—at all times, even when contact has been made, the kicker should keep his eyes locked onto the spot from where the ball was kicked and not the flight of the ball itself.

The reason why is simple. If you are going to watch the trajectory of the ball to see if the kick is good or not, you will inevitably begin to watch *at the moment of impact—before* you have completed the follow-through, with the leg snap that gives your boot that necessary extra-power lift-off. Checking the follow-through, experts insist, usually results in a hook or slice—and a wasted opportunity.

Instead, the kicker must wait until both of his feet have landed firmly on the ground, his kick effectively completed, before he raises his head to see whether his attempt at a field goal will be successful.

And whether the kicker is hitting the ball with his instep (soccer style) or with his toe, his target on the ball will always be the same: A point slightly beneath the halfway point on the vertical seam of the football. Again, the kicker actually watches his foot strike the ball, his eyes noting the moment of contact and then continuing to focus on the spot from which the ball was kicked.

It should be noted that the most common fault in placekicking, whether for an extra point or a field goal, but particularly in a long field-goal attempt—besides the tendency, built from anxiety, to guide the flight of the ball with your eyes and prayers—is the tendency of kickers to think that the harder they hit the ball, the farther it will go. As Garo Yepremian points out, that is not the case.

To begin with, the kicker should understand that technique and not power is what determines distance and accuracy.

Thus, he should understand that he will kick a 50-yard field goal and an attempt at conversion after touchdown in exactly the same way, exerting exactly the same degree of energy. The important thing is to hit the ball accurately which means observing the step-by-step mechanics of proper placekicking.

There is one difference, however. Although the force exerted is the same for a long or short placekick, for a field goal beyond the 40-yard line the kicker will aim at a point exactly in the center of the vertical seam of the football, or even slightly above it. The advantage of this is not distance or height *per se*, but a slower spin which tends to carry the ball farther, reducing wind resistance.

Says Minnesota's Fred Cox: I try to kick the ball from 20 yards the same as I would from 40. I don't try to kick the ball any harder until I get beyond the 45. It's not natural for me after that, and it strains my game."

It should also be reemphasized that no matter what style a kicker uses, no matter what angle he approaches the ball from, at the moment of kicking he brings his foot into the ball on a straight line terminating at the exact mid-center of the crossbar. When we see kickers taking those preliminary leg kicks before attempting the field goal or kickoff, they are in fact setting that imaginary—but real in their minds—bee-line toward the goal posts.

The sound of foot to ball is also an indication of how true will be the direction of the kick, says Cox. "I can tell if the ball is going through the bar the minute I kick it," he says. "The sound of the ball is entirely different. It cracks if I hit it well, but if I hear a dull thud I know I'm in trouble."

The kickoff varies from the field goal in minor respects only. The college kicker, who normally uses the kickoff tee for field-goal attempts, needs no adjusting to the kickoff, since the tee is permitted in pro ball and is generally employed. Kicking with the tee, of course, simplifies the mechanics of kicking enormously. In the

103

first place, it eliminates the snap from center, and the holder's need to position the ball properly. Eliminating the center and the holder from the operation reduces the possibilities for error—a bad snap, the holder taking too much time to set up or setting the ball at an awkward angle. Second, the tee reduces ground friction by giving the ball a smoother surface to rest on. Third, of course, the tee raises the ball two inches off the ground, giving the kicker a more visible target.

The other difference from field-goal kicking is in the length of approach to the ball. In kicking a field goal, the kicker must, as we have discussed, stand neither too far nor too near to his offensive blockers. The exact position of the older, we learned, is determined by the necessity to give the oncoming defensive backs awkward angles to the kick and kicker and simultaneously to permit the offensive linemen tight enough blocking angles to present a solid wall to rushing defensive linemen.

On the kickoff, of course, since the ball will not be in play until it is kicked, the kicker doesn't have to worry about pressure from his opponents. Therefore he usually takes a ten-yard run at the ball to build up additional momentum which, using the same easy motion as ever, he will translate into increased power at the moment of kicking.

Generally, however, he starts this run toward the ball at an easy trot, only turning on the speed over the last five yards.

Besides the field-goal attempt, try for point-after-touchdown and conventional kickoff, one other placekicking technique is employed often enough to merit discussion. The tactics, why and when, leading to its employment will be covered in the section on strategy.

The "squib kick" (often known by the name of a strategy for which it's often used—the onside kick) differs from all the others heretofore mentioned in that the ball, instead of being positioned upright at the time of the kick, is placed flat, with its longitudinal seam resting on the ground at a slight angle to the starting line. The squib kick, when executed properly, is low and difficult to handle, given its squibbling, erratic motion.

With the ball slightly angled and flat on the ground, the kicker generally kicks the ball at the point nearest him, right near the end of the football. If, instead of a low-line drive as required in an onside kick, the kicker wants to kick it over the heads of the first row of receivers, by kicking the ball near the center and getting under it he can loft the ball a considerable distance.

These then are the basic mechanics of placekicking. Once mastered, they constitute an art.

Says Jim Turner: "I stand in my own area at the end of the bench. People don't get too close to me. Sometimes the rookies will come over and say something at the beginning of the season, but they learn to leave me alone.

"In practice I check the wind in all parts of the field. I keep record of how it blows at different hours. I can tell you what the stadium grass is like in September and late and early October and every other time of the year. Look, this is my business, my bread and butter. One inch can mean a ballgame."

Easy???

16

THE ART OF PUNTING

Picture this: The team has a one-point advantage, but faces a fourth-down situation on its own goal line, 5 yards short of a first-down. Without an expert punter, the team is in deep trouble. Even a 50-yard kick with no run back will put the opponents in field-goal position. If, however, the team with the ball has a punter who can boot the ball 60 or more yards regularly and has proper downfield coverage from backs and linemen, the opposing ballcarrier can be brought down on his own 40—out of effective field-goal range.

Or even better: If the punter can not only kick for distance but for accuracy he will angle the punt out of bounds before a punt receiver has a chance to grab it, thus eliminating *any* chance for a game-breaking run back.

As the field-goal kicker has become the ultimate,

day-in-day-out, offensive weapon, the punter has come to play the same role for the defensive unit. When and where punting is used to best advantage will be discussed in our section on punting strategy. Suffice it to say that effective punting, combined with an adequate defense, can win games for a team whose offense is inferior to that of its opponent.

The most important prerequisites a successful punter must satisfy are consistency and elevation. Coaches must, with punting perhaps more than with any other football specialty, be able to call upon a punter knowing that he is going to kick, say, a minimum of 40-45 yards *every time* he is called upon to perform and that each of his kicks will be accurate—that is, placed for strategic advantage. A kicker who kicks 70-yarders one game and squibblers the next, or who kicks 70-yarders but has absolutely no idea where the kick is going to land, is of no use whatsoever. His inconsistency and unreliability disrupt the strategic flow of the game, and he will soon find himself benched in favor of athletes perhaps with less innate talent, but who have mastered the mechanics of punting.

Elevation is equally important. A 40-yard kick with good elevation is worth infinitely more than a 70-yard line drive. For a punt receiver will pick off the 70-yarder and have run back the kick for 40 yards—or perhaps even a touchdown—before the punting team can get downfield and set up for proper punt-defensive coverage. The kick elevation nullifies the possibility for a long return.

At the root of punting lies its fundamental purpose: to give the ball to the other team only in order to trap them in an unworkable field position. Punting is a strategic giveaway, in which a team A "lends" opponent B the ball for one series of downs, with the expectation that defense A will give it back to them four plays later, having gained a net yardage advantage.

There is more flexibility in punting styles than in placekicking styles, so that the differences in styles are often compared to those between hitters in baseball. But whether the bat is held high over the shoulder, whether a batter crowds the plate, stands back to the rear or forward, whether he grips the bat near the end or chokes up four inches, there are some basic rules all batters obey. No baseball player who expects to hit the ball takes his eyes off it while it is in flight. Every good hitter tries to meet the ball with the fat part of the bat. Every hitter, except in special situations, tries to make contact off a level swing.

Likewise, there are a set of invariable mechanics in punting. Despite the apparent discrepancies of style, the basics of punting are a routine that every punter who hopes to be successful will succeed in dominating.

It's surprising how many kids trying to punt tend to think of that activity as strictly dependent on a natural talent. They pick up the ball, take as many steps as they feel are necessary and kick it. The next time they kick, they may take one step less in their approach, may kick the ball from a slightly different angle—and are surprised when the ball reacts differently.

And yet, the key to good punting is repetition. The basics must be mastered, and once mastered, the punter must stick to them with slavish fealty. Since the punter, once he receives the snap from center, is operating strictly on his own, there is no reason why he should not get off his best kick every single time.

Before he ever gets on the football field, there are ways to tell whether a candidate has some of the essential ingredients necessary for a punter. For example, coaches often use blindfold tests to determine if a player has the prime prerequisite of a punter: excellent balance.

In the Mills test the potential punter walks 50 yards in a straight line, then is blindfolded and told to walk the same 50-yard straight line again. No one, of course, is going to walk the line blindfolded without going at least somewhat off course. But by noting how much the player deviates, the coach can gain some insight into his innate sense of balance. If, for example, the candidate walks in a circle instead of a bee-line, he's not going to have the built-in homing device so necessary for good punting. Furthermore, the test also permits coach and player to see which side the player's natural drift is. The player will then work to eliminate the drift, which he is usually unaware of until shown.

Again, as in placekicking, a player who panics is not suited to the role of punter, when the total activity on a single play focuses on him when every member of the opposing unit is trying to tackle him before he can get off his kick.

Perhaps the pressure in punting is even greater than that endured by the field-goal kicker. In almost every case, unless the field-goal kicker has completely botched his boot or is attempting to kick one beyond his normal range, the ball—if unsuccessful—will have crossed the end zone and will be brought out to his opponent's 20-yard line.

The punter, however, will, unless he kicks coffin-corner

for the sidelines, almost always face some kind of run back. Thus he must be just as accurate in terms of distance as the field-goal kicker, and perhaps even *more* accurate in terms of placement, and doubly concerned with elevation.

Of course, there are pressure points in field-goal kicking not endured by the punter, so the pressures even out. The point here is that it's well to remember that punting is more than dropping a ball onto the foot, kicking it upfield and waving it goodbye. Punting is a craft. It requires discipline, nerve and the stringing of a series of small integral movements into a fluid totality, whose *end result only* is the kick itself and follow through.

One of the major differences between punting and placekicking is that the punter must have one more skill than the man who makes his living solely by his toe or instep. The punter must, above all, be able to catch a football; he is, in effect, his own holder. All the responsibilities that in placekicking are shared by the holder—catching and positioning the ball at the proper angle, with the laces facing in the proper direction, rest in punting on the man who will do the kicking.

Thus, he must be aware from the beginning of the center's responsibilities, what he can expect from his center, what errors of judgment he must be prepared for. So he must be aware that the center, often confronted on a punting situation with a blitzing defensive lineman intent on spoiling the kick, is often more concerned with his blocking assignment than whether his pass to the punter is directly on target.

In theory, of course, the center's primary responsibility is to get that pass back accurately. In practice, however, operating in the pit, his first instinct may be toward preservation.

Furthermore, the punter has to *know* the game of football. A punter who has had experience at a ball-handling position like quarterback, halfback or wide receiver is a tremendous tactical asset to his team. If the pass back from center is way off target, this type of punter can then exercise an option to run, especially in a fourth-down situation where only short yardage is required for a first down.

If he is granted that option by his coaches, or if the snap is so far off the mark that running is his only option, he must possess two other qualities necessary to every football player who actually handles the ball in game situations. On a deviant snap, even if he does not exercise the option to run, he must have the instinct and savvy to move with the ball. Oncoming linemen or safeties will be attempting to cut through his kicking angle, forcing him to vacate his habitual kicking spot. The expert punter, in that situation, as unpleasant as it may be for the coaches who have carefully worked out their clockwork strategy, must be able to fake oncoming defenders effectively, moving out of their way and still getting off his kick. Unlike placekicking, the punter is often called on to react in a spontaneous way to unexpected situations.

Again, the pressures are similar to those endured by quarterbacks, but with this crucial difference: If the quarterback cannot find receivers downfield to throw to, he still has options—safety-valve plays involving other backs. At worst, he can simply drop to the ground, somewhere near the scrimmage line, knowing that he can still call upon his kickers to get him out of a hole on fourth down.

The punter, on the other hand, knows full well that he is only called upon when all other options have been used up. If his kick is blocked and recovered by the other team, they can run the ball in for a touchdown. (And since most blocked punts do occur behind the line of scrimmage, the charging offensive linemen can often give the kind of protection to the man who picked up the ball that allows him to ramble on for a long gain.) Once, say, an Alan Page blocks the ball, with a Carl Eller shadowing him protectively, it takes the skills of a linebacker or safety to catch and bring him down. And they, of course, in a punting situation, would usually be sitting on the sidelines.

In sum, the punt receiver should have the attitude that safety organizations advocate for automobile drivers. The driver, they suggest, should constantly expect other drivers to make errors and should condition his driving accordingly. Likewise, the punter should always expect the worst from his center—he should always be mentally prepared for a snap that is off target.

As in placekicking, balance is a crucial factor in whether a punt will be successful or not. Of course, the great virtuoso punters can kick off balance under pressure, or at least when they seem to be off balance. Despite appearances, however, at the moment they begin their kicking motion they are in perfect balance, no matter what unpredicted maneuvers they have gone through to get into that perfectly balanced stance.

When the punter enters the game, he generally positions himself about 15 yards in back of the center, the distance being determined by the need to give the punter time to get his kick off before it is blocked. In pro football, coaches expect their centers to get the ball to the punter in between 8/10 to 9/10ths of a second.

To get a bird's-eye view of how important timing is, spend some time watching a coach in practice. He'll be using a stopwatch to time two different factors: the length of time the punted ball hangs in the air and the time it takes between the center's snap and the sound of the kick. Either of these factors can count more than the yardage the kick travels. If a punt hangs in the air 4.6 to 5.0 seconds, it's good timing.

"The quicker the ball gets to the receiver," Vince Lombardi liked to warn his punters, "the quicker it gets back"—meaning the returner will bring it back for more yardage against the kicking team.

Once he's at the proper distance from the scrimmage line and properly lined up behind the man who will pass the ball to him, the punter takes his stance. First, he should position his feet with the kicking foot slightly ahead of the non-kicking foot. However, although almost every expert recommends this juxtaposition of the feet, you will notice at high school and college levels—and even, although rarely, at the professional level—that some kickers line up with the non-kicking foot in front of the kicking foot.

The reason why this is not advisable is very simple: Starting from this position adds an extra step, or steps, before booting the ball—requiring more time to get the kick off, and putting the punter closer to the line of scrimmage, where those beefy linemen are desparately anxious to smother his attempt.

Technically, the difference reduces to this: If the kicker who positions his non-kicking foot first leads off with that foot, he must take a full two and a half steps before punting the ball; when he takes his first step from that position with his kicking foot, he still needs two steps before he kicks the ball. However, the punter who stands with his kicking foot forward can kick the ball after only having taken one and a half steps. That half-step saved puts the punter a half-step in front of the charging linemen.

The kicker stands with his hands loose and relaxed at his sides, his body angled slightly forward. The palms of his hands are held up, with the thumbs out, to give the center a large target. As in every type of kicking, where the kicker puts his gaze is as important as where he places his foot. The standard phrase used among players and coaches alike is a specific enough direction: Look the ball into your hands. The elbows should be bent slightly, so that the hands can be cupped to receive the ball. In making the "cup," the hand that is going to be placed under the ball should be positioned forward of the hand that is going to be held over the ball. The fingers should be spread apart, stretching the cup to its maximum dimensions.

The cup formed by the hands, of course, must be positioned in line with the center's target. The center will be aiming at the inside part of the punter's right thigh, and the punter should hold his hands before, and slightly below, this target area (below, to compensate for the natural rise of the center's pass).

There are also rules to be observed in catching the center's pass, rules which if not observed inhibit the punter's total movement. First of all, when catching the ball the punter must resist the temptation to pull the ball back toward his body. This would present an extra movement, as the punter will be kicking the ball with his arms extended. If the pass is off target, which is exactly what the punter with a proper attitude will be anticipating, the punter should not move just his arms over in the direction of the pass, but should move his entire body in front of it.

The reasons for moving the entire body are twofold: First, if the pass is low he can trap it against his body, reducing the possibility of a fumble; second, by moving his entire body, he can keep his feet in position to begin his punt, without losing the balance necessary to get off a good boot.

What is the proper position for the punter's feet? Generally, the punter places his kicking foot down then lines up his non-kicking foot with the toe coming up to the instep of the kicking foot. But there is no fixed rule here; lining up the toe of the non-kicking foot at the instep is a general guideline which—like the width of the punter's stance—is adaptable to the comfort of the kicker. One factor which does not vary, however, is how the punter lines up his kicking foot, the direction he points that foot. The kicker points his foot directly at the middle of the center's body.

When a punter is not kicking away, but angling for a specific point on the sidelines and out of bounds, or directing his kick at a specific receiver, he may alter his position.

Angling the kick to the left, for example, the punter would move a little to the right, then angle his body to the left.

Many coaches object to this tactic on strategic grounds. By deliberately angling his body in the direction he's going to kick, they argue, the kicker is telling the defenders exactly where he plans to boot the ball.

In summary, common sense dictates that when there is no strategic advantage to be lost by telegraphing the kick, angling his body toward the place he wants to put the ball may be advisable. In every other case, the kicker should take a stance squared off with the center, as previously explained.

Now the potential punter knows everything he needs to know, except what to do with the ball when he catches it.

17

HOW TO PUNT

The ball, of course, is held parallel to the ground. Whether the laces are tilted up or toward either side is irrelevant, as long as the punter can see them. The one thing he does not want to do is kick the ball on the laces, which will send the ball along an erratic trajectory.

The older method called for the punter to drop his left hand away quickly as he dropped the ball for the kick. With his left hand then available for balancing his body, the punter had the ball controlled by his right hand, with the seam below lined up with the punter's middle finger. When he dropped the ball, the punter had merely to "take his right hand away."

The major advantage for this system, it is argued, is that when the kicker lowers the ball, it is being held by one hand only. It's impossible to retain your balance and retain good punting form while lowering the ball with both hands. This method allows the punter to use his left hand for balancing, while he merely has to lower his right hand toward his leg.

Many modern experts disapprove of this method, however, because it often leads to the end-over-end kick. These strategists prefer their punters to try for spiral kicks, and to obtain the spiral, the punter must slant the ball downward, which is best accomplished by dropping the ball onto the foot with both hands clamped to the sides of it.

Another alternative is a combination of the two methods, in which the punter drops the ball onto his foot with one hand, yet manages to turn the tip down at the same time, the resulting kick being a spiral.

Most kickers today use the two-handed method, in which the right hand goes near the top face of the ball, while the left and guiding hand is near the front of it. When the ball is dropped, both hands merely fall away, reducing the friction attendant to other methods where the right hand must be slid out from under the ball. The hands, especially the left, act, it should be noted, like a frame; the left hand does not grip, but merely is there for stability.

As soon as the punter gets the ball, he must start his pattern of steps. That initial step is merely a break into movement—what experts call a "comfort" step, directly at the target the punter is aiming for. As the terminology indicates, the comfort step should be neither too short, nor too long. The punter must be moving in a relaxed manner and must be in good balance throughout.

The second step, with the non-kicking foot, follows naturally. Here again the punter must strive not to *over*step or else his punt is likely to lack elevation sufficient to clear the outstretched arms of defenders and provide adequate time for proper kick-return coverage. This second step should be in the same direction as the first; the difference between second and first steps is that the first step provides direction, the second momentum and power.

The steps, of course, must become routine. There's a similarity here to the steps hurdlers take, forward but with the emphasis on finding a rhythm suitable to one's height, weight and physique, then practicing that movement over and over again until the rhythm becomes second nature to you—*your* rhythm every single time you punt. The punter who has to worry about the mechanics of kicking will inevitably make errors.

The situation he enters the game with will vary; the direction of his kick will vary; on certain occasions he will not even be able to kick from the spot he has chosen, due to pressure put on him by the defense. Yet if the rhythms of punting have internalized, from whatever point he does finally kick, he will do so with proper technique.

Just as he is about to take his last step, the punter drops the ball onto his kicking foot. The idea is to get the ball flat on your foot, with the front tip of the ball tilting slightly downward. If the rear tip is down instead, that tends to be the part of the ball that meets the punter's foot, resulting as we've noted before, in an undesirable end-over-end kick.

With the ball dropping, the kicking leg comes up like a

pendulum to meet it. The left hand—the guiding hand—has released the ball first, simply by pulling away from the pigskin's surface. The idea is to keep the right hand on the ball as long as possible before making contact with the foot.

The ball must be placed in front of the kicker, on an imaginary line from the hip of the kicker's punting leg onto the spot he's aiming for. And perhaps most important of all—and most often forgotten—the punter must hold the ball far enough away from his body, in an outward direction, so that his leg can kick through the full pendulum sequence. Far enough away from the body to permit accurate kicking, remember, but not so far away that the right hand has to let the ball go too soon in order to meet the upcoming foot.

The greater the distance the ball falls through the air from that right hand, the greater the chance that the ball will deviate from course, and result in a bad kick. Most ineffective punts are the result of a bad drop on the part of the punter, so this aspect of the punter's technique deserves particular care.

As that left leg hits the ground and the right leg comes forward, in rhythm to the descent of the right hand, about to drop the ball, the knee of the kicking leg should be bent as much as possible to provide a spring of power for the kick. Not, as we've pointed out before, that the kicker should try to "kill" the ball. An over-aggressive approach usually leads to a worthless kick. Instead of crashing the foot into the ball, the desired action is a whip-like snap, with the toe of the kicking foot pointing down.

It is at this point that balance comes into play—and the

punter must have the balance of a tight-rope walker. For with one foot (the non-kicking foot) planted on the ground and the other foot snapping out to kick the ball, the punter is effectively balancing on one leg. And it is at this point that he may succumb to a "disease" native to punters only—"punter's drift."

Earlier, we mentioned that coaches often use a blindfold test, making the potential punter walk 50 yards in as straight a line as possible, in order, in part, to determine their natural "drift." In general, though, the natural tendency of the kicker who boots with his right foot will be a rightward drift, while the leftfooted punter will drift toward the left. If unchecked, these wayward drifts will produce punts that deviate correspondingly.

The main way to combat these drifts is to make sure that when positioning the feet before punting, the drift is not built into the stance. The feet, as we've previously noted, should point straight ahead (unless, of course, the punter is intentionally setting out to angle the ball). Starting out in proper position, he must make sure that his subsequent steps do not deviate from that position, that he does not let the "drift" infiltrate his approach toward kicking the ball.

Finally, having mastered his approach to the ball, having learned how to drop the ball onto his foot properly, the kicker is ready for the fundamentals of contact with the ball. The toe, remember, has been positioned flat out and downward. The aim of contact is to place the ball just to the outside of the right arch (assuming, for instructional purposes, a right-footed kicker). Experienced kickers insist that they can "feel" a good kick by the pressure contact exerts at the middle of the instep.

The ball, on the other hand, should be kicked a little behind its midpoint. In other words: Fat part of ball meets fat part of foot. Neither the toes nor the ankle should ever come in contact with the ball on a punt.

But the syndrome doesn't end here; it's not enough merely to set into proper motion, take the necessary steps and kick the ball accurately. For without a convincing follow-through the punt will totter, then sink like a bird with a broken wing.

We said that the ball is kicked off a leg snap, with the bent knee now springing straight out to provide the motive power. For follow-through, we should emphasize that the leg continues through the kicking arc until the knee locks—the leg carrying through to a height usually above the kicker's head.

While he is actually kicking, of course, the kicker's back will be bent. But as his leg climbs through the air, his back straightens and his shoulders are thrown back, providing the maximum amount of power for the kick. In no case should the non-kicking foot ever leave the ground, however. Although leaping with the non-kicking foot off the ground does provide more motive power, it detracts from the punter's balance and therefore may affect his accuracy adversely.

Besides, the punter—like the placekicker—must keep his head down while he kicks, his eyes locked on the ball up to and including the moment when his foot makes contact. But when the non-kicking foot leaves the ground, the natural tendency is for the punter to lift his head up and therefore break his concentration before he has completed his follow-through.

Interestingly enough, how you land at the completion of your kick is a good indicator as to how successful your attempt at punting has been. Someone well-versed in the mechanics of punting, in fact, when permitted to view only the punter's post-kick stance, can predict with accuracy what kind of punt the kicker managed to execute. In fact, the feet, with relation to each other, should mirror the pre-punt stance with regard to relative position and the distance between them. If, for example, your feet are not parallel after kicking, we can surmise that your kick has deviated from the planned path.

Needless to say, at the moment of kicking, the punter is really moving forward with the momentum, and should, after completing his follow-through, advance a step or two forward to eliminate the possibility of an awkward rollback. If, however, he has executed every other link in the chain of technique, these steps forward will be automatic.

The aim of the kick, of course, is a good spiral, rather than an end-over-end. Modern kickers prefer the spiral for one reason: The spiral action allows the ball—when all other effects are equal—to carry farther through the air and at a much greater elevation. If the procedures outlined up to now are strictly observed, the good spiral will automatically result. If the kicker finds he is producing a "floater," an end-over-end or a nose-up spiral, then he must work to correct whatever mistakes he's making.

These errors usually can be traced back either to improper positioning of the ball at the drop, improper leg motion at the instant of kicking or the fact that the punter is kicking the ball with the wrong part of his foot.

The end-over-end effect usually occurs when the punter is kicking the ball with his toes in an upward direction; this "cupping" effect produces a topsy-turvy reaction. It's undesirable because the ball will only travel for short distances and may bounce erratically when it hits the ground. Often the bounce is back toward the direction from which the ball was kicked, losing the valuable yardage the punter had gained through the air.

The floater, on the other hand, is the kick you get when you try to kick the ball with your leg—as opposed to the smooth motion we have outlined that involves the coordination of back, shoulders, knee, ankle and arms. Novices are prone to produce floaters. They operate on the erroneous premise that the harder they kick the ball, the farther it will travel. A "smash," however, produces only the floater—a flight pattern inferior to the spiral due to its inability to cut through wind resistance.

The nose-up spiral results when the kicker boots the ball near its tip. Again, this kick is bound to travel a shorter distance because it provides in its flight pattern more surface for the wind to work against.

Remember that the use of the spiral is not just for greater distance. The spiral motion itself keeps the ball on course, and will resist atmospheric factors that would otherwise act to change the kick's direction.

Two specialized punts that we will be discussing in our chapter on punting strategy deserve some consideration here, as their execution differs in slight detail from the normal punt. The coffin-corner is a kick that expert punters will attempt for strategic reasons. Effectively, it means kicking the ball so that it will go out of bounds at a preselected spot, usually deep in an opponent's territory. The aim here is usually to place the ball out of bounds within five yards of the goal posts the opponents are defending, eliminating a runback, and at the same time restricting their offense to simple straight-ahead plays that can be easily read by your own defense.

In a kick like this, where pin-point accuracy is demanded, the most important factor the kicker should concern himself with is the natural pull or draw inherent in all punters. In this situation, the kicker must take the snap and advance through his steps directly at the spot he hopes to intersect with his kick. He must make sure he has compensated for that natural pull that makes the kicks of lefties veer to the left and those of righties to the right.

The quick kick is also used to good effect in special situations. Here the essential problem for the punter is one of timing. He must take the snap and get into the proper kicking position at the very same moment, as the effectiveness of the quick kick depends on the element of surprise. As soon as he has the ball in his hands, he is beginning his kicking motion.

The quick kick is usually a low kick, so the punter must remember to drop the ball a little lower than normal before striking it. He should also hold back slightly on his follow-through. As with every type of punter, though, before deciding on how he is going to kick the ball, the punter must know something about what effect a prevailing wind will have on it.

Every field has its idiosyncracies, special mysteries which the punter must unravel and which knowledge he must then include in his mental preparations for kicking. The slope of the ground, whether the turf is artificial or natural, with their differing potentialities for friction, lighting, all these factors must be considered before the punter puts his foot into the ball. The most important consideration of all, however, is the wind or air currents which may operate to change the direction of his punt.

The key to dealing with variations in the intensity and direction of wind is compensation. A headwind, naturally, will reduce the distance and velocity of the spiral, while sometimes tending to hold the ball in the air longer than would be normal. A tailwind, on the other hand, will tend to increase the ball's velocity and often affect its elevation. A crosswind moving past the body in the direction of the kicking leg (left to right for a rightfooted kicker, for example) means simply that the kicker's natural pull to the left will probably be canceled out, and he must compensate for that lack of customary pull. A crosswind blowing past his body away from the kicking leg, however, will accentuate the punter's natural pull or draw, again making compensation necessary.

How does the punter learn what to do, what to expect in any given situation? He must experiment and ask the advice of those more experienced than himself. Picking the brain of an experienced coach or fellow punter, he's likely to turn up gems of information about weather, turf and the peculiarities of the particular fields and stadiums he's expected to perform in.

The final factor the punter must be aware of in order not only to execute his kick properly, but to play his part in the team's overall strategy, is concerned with "time." In fact, most blocked punts are due to the kicker taking too much time before getting off his kick. The rapidity with which a punter gets away his kick is considered of such overriding importance, in fact, that experts have determined to the nearest tenth of a second the maximum time allowable for a punter's kick to have any chance of being successful.

Including the pass from center, the kicker's reception and punt, the permissible elapsed interval has been computed at *two seconds*. If the team is punting from a closed punt-formation, a kick within 1.8 seconds after the snap from center is desirable, if possible, given the relative expertise of center and punter. If, however, the punter is operating behind a spread punt-formation, the total permissible time is not more than 2.3 seconds.

Times over those computed, the coaches and expert punters argue, may often result in blocked punts. The computations, of course, are based on a number of factors: How long it takes for the snap from center, then the kick, correlated with the time interval for which linemen can be expected to hold to their blocking assignments.

Of course, these times are out of reach for the beginner; they are an ultimate goal, but still they point out an interesting fact: In order to achieve these times, both the center and the punter must dominate their respective positions. These two positions together must cooperate to the fullest if a punt is to be successful.

Now we have the fundamentals both of placekicking and punting. But telling a potential punter or placekicker how to kick still leaves the question of when and where unanswered. In the following section we'll analyze the strategies that have made these two forms of kicking so important to the modern game.

18

WHEN TO PUNT

The name of the game in modern football is "ball control." The notion is a very obvious one. The team that is able to keep possession of the ball for the largest duration of game time is doing so by its ability to run and pass the ball to advantage. A team that *cannot* retain control of the football is giving its opponents a chance to use their offensive weapons.

Fundamentally, then, punting is something a coach must have at hand for those moments when his offense is not able to dominate by passing or running, when ball control is an impossibility. The overall rating of the various aspects of the game, in fact, is illustrated by teams like the Minnesota Vikings and the Miami Dolphins. Stress with these teams is placed on defense first, then the kicking game and finally offense. In the era of ball control and defensive football, the kicking game is of primary concern.

Yet there are two distinct kinds of punting situations. In one, the punting team expects to obtain some kind of immediate offensive advantage. The other is a purely defensive maneuver, preventing the opponent's offense from getting possession of the ball in too advantageous a field position.

The offensive punt most often used is what is call the quick kick. Here a team punts on an early down, when the defense is obviously prepared for the pass or run, not the kick. The idea is to get the ball far enough down field to place your opponent in dangerous field position. Of course, if *your* defense is weak, the offensive punt is useless, for the opponent will merely drive right back upfield.

The defensive punt is the one the kicker is most often called upon to execute. This time the offensive team kicks on fourth down, usually from deep in its own territory. With the offensive punt the linemen are sent downfield immediately, but with the defensive punt the opponent is ready for the kick and is usually trying to block it. Therefore the punting team's linemen are around the scrimmage line, forming a tight blocking wall. At the kick, they're downfield trying to limit the opponent's run back.

It's worth noting here that when we say "ball control" we are imbuing the term with a subtler definition than it had, say, a decade ago. Ball control now includes the idea of "field position"—and thus the importance of punting is stressed. By this we mean that modern coaches are not reluctant to give up the ball, if they can hope to get it back in good field position, *and* quickly. Thus from 50 yards on into the enemy's territory, most coaches will not hesitate to punt if they think they can gain more than from a pass or a run.

In the past, of course, the concept of ball control meant hold onto it as long as possible, irrespective of field position. Thus, when Sammy Baugh punted, it was only as a defensive last resort or as a quickly executed surprise. Not so today.

The most important rule underlying the defensive punting strategy is: Punt on fourth down every time a loss of downs would create a dangerous field advantage for the opponents. A punter must understand this. He must kick that ball every time the coach or quarterback calls for the punt in that fourth-down situation. A bad pass from center, oncoming linemen who chase the punter away from his kicking spot, no matter what unforeseen circumstance crops up at the moment, the punter *must* get his kick away. A poor kick is better than no kick at all.

Sometimes, of course, a punter can barely repress the image of himself as a potential Gale Sayers. All of us, undoubtedly, harbor within the urge to tuck that ball in our guts and dazzle a defense with our fancy footwork. But it's a fatal flaw for a punter.

The idea here, of course, is to get the ball as near to your opponent's goal line as possible. By doing so, the kicking team effectively bunches up the opponent's offense. The opponent will hesitate to try a forward pass from in close to his goal line, because an interception would probably lead to a touchdown. He will hesitate to send his running backs on end sweeps for fear of a major loss or a safety. His only options are straight-ahead or narrow-angle plunges.

When teams are of more or less equal strengths, quarterbacks should be aware that to pass or sweep near their own goal line is to defy the odds of probability. And good teams try to make the odds work for them. Gambling is a last resort, the final refuge of a weak team.

A word here about the coffin-corner technique, whose mechanics we described earlier. The coffin-corner, where a punter aims to put the ball out of bounds right near his opponent's goal line, is rarely used at any level above high school football. Not that there aren't kickers around who can send the ball out of bounds fairly consistently within their opponent's ten-yard line. But sometimes even they miss. The reason the coffin-corner has gone out of fashion has to do with the kinds of punt-return formations now in use. A punt to one side of the field allows the receiving unit to concentrate all its forces in that area. The punt-receiving unit, of course, merely has to move laterally to set up its return formation, while the kicking unit has to move downfield. Therefore the punt-return unit has plenty of time to set up, creating a solid phalanx of defenders for the punt returner.

While we said before that the line punter should never deviate from the play called in the huddle and that once he is ordered to punt, he punts no matter what the obstacle, there is one situation in which the punter lines up in punt formation, but does not kick.

The fake punt is a maneuver that requires long experience on the part of the punter. In this case, the punter is either instructed to run the play in the huddle, or is given the option to run it *if* conditions are favorable.

134

Usually, in a fake-punt situation, the punter will run rather than pass. A pass pattern has to be preplanned because it involves coordinating the passer's movements with the actions of so many other players. And planning strategy with members of a special team who are only in a ball game to execute the punt can lead to a devastating and chaotic mixup. Some experts argue, in fact, that the fake kick is usually most successful not when it's called in a huddle, but when it "happens" at the line of scrimmage.

At the pro level perhaps. At the high school and college levels a fake kick should only be executed when called for by the coach or quarterback. Otherwise the punter should kick, no matter what the pressure. Pressure is simply something he has to learn to live with.

The aim of the fake punt, of course, is to catch your opponent by surprise. He expect you to kick and is gearing his defense toward it. In a short yardage situation, the punter may be able to get the first down.

There are two moments when the fake punt is relevant:

1. When a team is far ahead, a fake punt can demoralize its opponent even further. But it should only be attempted when the kicking team has already crossed its fifty yard line.

2. When a team is behind, it may elect to go to the fake punt in desperation if there's little game time remaining.

In either case it's a calculated risk which may backfire. A fake punt that fails can steal the momentum away from the team punting, especially a fake punt which hasn't been called in the huddle. The punter's teammates, for example, may well resent the kicker's initiative; their resentment may grow to sullenness, then desperation and disinterest.

Football today is a clockwork game in which individual and intricate maneuvers are synchronized to obtain a specific objective. Initiative at the wrong time can shatter completely a team's coherence.

In executing the punt, the kicker is usually expected to kick not only for distance, but for height. The high kick is intended to keep the runback to a minimum. While a punter is judged by the distance of his kick, a more effective measurement of the entire punting unit is the distance the kick travels, minus the yardage the kick is run back. In fact, the punter who gets his kick away quickest and *makes the ball stay up in the air longest* is the most effective. A towering 40-yard spiral is often more useful than a 70-yard line drive. The punt returner has a chance to take that 70-yard line drive all the way back to his opponent's goal line. The skyscraping 40-yarder, on the other hand, will result in a "fair catch," eliminating the possibility of any return at all.

One of the most challenging situations for a punter is when he's forced to kick out of his own end zone. Usually, of course, a punter kicks from anywhere up to about fifteen yards back of scrimmage. When an end zone kick is called for, a punter must make some difficult adjustments. For if in making his approach or setting up for his kick the punter steps on or beyond the rear end-zone line, it's an automatic safety, and two points for the other team.

So with the ball set, say, on the 1-yard line, the maximum distance the kicker can stand away from it is 11 yards. The kicker has to work faster, and under increased pressure. He knows that a blocked kick in the end zone may very well lead to a touchdown for his opponents at

136

worst or a safety against his own team.

His chances for getting off a good punt are also limited by the fact that at the end zone his linemen have to line up tighter than usual, to eliminate all loopholes in the blocking alignments. So when he does get his kick off, he can count on it being run back farther than usual. Because a blocked punt can lead to a touchdown, the linemen will give the kicker longer protection, but will thereby get downfield later. The longer the kick, in fact, the easier it is to return for the opposing safetyman. He will have such a jump on your downfield linemen that by the time they reach him he will already have a full head of steam up.

The best tactic when kicking from the end zone is to aim for a coffin-corner placement. For this kind of kick, the end zone is the best place on the field. The end zone, for example, is the one part of the field in which the kicker can ask the official to move the ball, at least in professional football. If, for example, the kicker's view is blocked by the goal post, with a possibility that the ball might bounce off the crossbar or uprights in its takeoff, he can ask the official to set the ball down either to the right or left (but never forward) in order to facilitate his view and the flight of the ball.

In college, of course, where the goal posts are located exactly on the end-zone lines, the kicker must kick from wherever the official places the ball. His main task is to remember never to step across or onto that rear end-zone line, which would result in a gift two points for his opponents.

Traditionally, there are two basic formations used in kicking a punt. Let's discuss first the "spread" or "open" punt formation and its variations. The easiest way to recognize a spread from a closed formation, of course, is that in the closed formation the punter is crowding his center, not the 13 to 15 yards back so common in the modern game. But although the spread or one of its variations is most often used at every level of competition, the closed does have some advantages which we'll discuss in a moment.

The aim of course of all punting formations is to give the kicker adequate protection first, then permit blockers to easily turn into hunters, charging downfield to eliminate any return, preventing the opponent from reducing the overall yardage of the punt. Those players who are not required to protect the kick, of course, leave at the snap of the ball. The ends stream straight downfield, crashing through blockers to drive the return away from the sidelines. The backs are also on the outside, with the linemen spread across the middle. The aim is lateral coverage, with players creating a solid wall of defenders right across the width of the field.

In the spread formation, the linemen are set with wider gaps between them than in other formations. Here the crucial burden rests on the center to get his pass back not only accurately but very quickly to the punter, who is positioned 13 to 15 yards behind scrimmage. The advantage here is that the linemen are not required to hold their blocks very long, since the punter is standing so deep. Furthermore, the linemen are already fanned out at scrimmage, and are in much better position to limit the yardage of the punt return.

Experts are in general agreement that despite the fact

that the punter is kicking from up to 5 yards farther back than in closed formations, the net yardage of the kick will be greater. The kick may be shorter, but in proportion, the runback will be comparatively small.

The closed punt-formation is set up more or less like a conventional play from scrimmage. The linemen are shoulder to shoulder. As opposed to the spread, where a lineman blocks man to man, the closed formation requires that the linemen fill gaps, leaving no porous crack for a defensive player to slip through. The advantage is that the kicker gets maximum protection; the disadvantage is that linemen are late (compared with expectations from the spread punt-formation) covering the kick return.

The punter must be able to adapt to any formation. But adaptation should be easy, for the variables of his trade are constant, the mechanics the same no matter how far from scrimmage he stands, no matter how the teammates in front of him are lining up.

19

WHEN TO PLACEKICK

The rise of the field-goal kicker to prominence in the modern game has little to do with fashion or even the influx of soccer stylists claiming more accurate and longer kicks. In fact, placekicking has become more important in proportion to the growth and effectiveness of new defensive alignments.

Decades ago, for example, on a fourth-down situation, a team that was losing with scant game time remaining had only one alternative to running with the ball: the long bomb, the go-for-broke pass that would reverse its fortunes.

However, in these days of zone defenses, where pass defenders are not restricted to one-to-one coverage and will help out on a pass receiver committed to a specific zone of the playing field, the "bomb" more often than not injures the team that tries to employ it, rather than its opponents. The interception, with its attendant runback possibilities, makes the bomb a chancy proposition. Its use today is restricted primarily to those situations in which it is least expected, say, third down and inches to go for a first down. Even then, of course, it's a strategic gamble, a calculated risk undertaken in the waning moments of the game when more than three points are needed to tie or win.

At least at the professional level, then, the bread-and-butter strategy for accumulating points when they are needed in a hurry is to call upon the field-goal kicker. And more and more, as coaches become aware of the necessity for proper instructional tools for turning out placekickers, the specialists are coming to the forefront at the college and even high school levels.

But the rise to prominence of the field goal in today's football strategy has produced an important corollary too often overlooked: if the field goal is not successful, the kicking team winds up in a much worse situation than if it had elected to do something besides kick.

Thus, the decision whether to go for a field goal or not is a crucial one. Before making that decision, a number of factors must be taken into account.

It is obvious that the strength of the kicker is an all-important consideration. A placekicker who has difficulty booting the ball 40 yards, say, will not be called upon to try a 50-yarder, unless the alternative is sure defeat.

Weather will also play a part in the decision. A strong wind blowing at the kicker reduces his distance in direct proportion to its velocity. A strong crosswind will also provide for complications. Rain or snow will create the slippery, unpredictable conditions that increase the possibilities for error.

And after all those automatic decisions have been made, the kicker, his coach and quarterback have to think about the specific situation in the game at hand. The score, field position at the moment of the kick, the relative strengths of the kicker's offensive line against his opponent's defense, what down he will enter the game on, these are some of the questions that must be answered before a team can risk opting for the field goal.

Basically, a team goes for the field goal when it needs three points. Of course, since no lead is ever big enough, a team is always in need of three more points, so the prime question reduces to the elements we've discussed up to now, with the additional factor of downs.

Fundamentally, the placekick is a fourth-down maneuver. There is no point of trying it on an earlier down. The element of surprise that makes a quick-punt successful on first down is lacking. The formation makes it obvious that you are aiming for the field goal.

Besides, a field goal is less than half the points awarded for a touchdown and extra point. Strategy dictates its use when it seems doubtful that a team can advance unimpeded toward a touchdown.

The field goal is not, however, a last resort. As we've noted in this day of zone coverage, quarterbacks can no longer count on scoring six quick points by throwing the bomb. Thus the field goal may be the quickest and safest way to put points on the scoreboard. Furthermore, a team without a superior running and passing attack still has a chance to win with its placekicker. If it can get past midfield, say, four times during the game, a decent field-goal kicker should convert between half and three-quarters of those drives into scores, depending on the distance he kicks from.

Placekicking in college presents a further option to the team lining up in field-goal formation. Under college rules, the holder is permitted to catch the football, position it while he makes contact with the ground with his knee, and then get up and pass or run with the ball. If used when the defense is off-guard, this fake field goal can be an effective surprise play.

While it's obvious to even the casual fan that attempting or not attempting a field goal in any given situation is a complex strategic decision, at the same time most fans are not aware of the various strategies available on the *kickoff*. The strategic decisions begin right after the coin toss.

The team that wins the coin toss does not always elect to receive. Why? The wind may be blowing against the direction his offense will have to move in. On the other hand, a strong wind advantage can be a tremendous aid, not only to the kicker but his quarterback's passes. When there is a wind advantage, the winner of the coin toss usually elects to receive.

In special situations, the on-side kick can be an important alternative to the conventional kickoff. The timing for it is usually the closing minutes of a game, when the team kicking off is down by anywhere up to seven points. There is time enough for a field goal or touchdown, but only if the kicking team recovers possession of the football immediately. Or, reversing the situation, your team may be *ahead* by a small margin in the closing minutes. If you have to kick, and are skeptical about the ability of your defense to contain the opposing offense, you might elect for the onside kick, hoping to regain possession and run out the clock.

In either case, with the ball laid flat on its side, the kicker usually boots a low line drive that bounces off a lineman. Since linemen are unaccustomed to fielding kickoffs, there is a good possibility that a fumble will occur, and that the kicking team will recover its own boot. The kick must, of course, travel at least ten yards before it is in play.

One further word on the kickoff. Just as kicking has become the domain of specialists, running back kicks has likewise become an art. Kick returners are inevitably speedballs, with good hands, who are expert open-field runners and yet masters of using their protection to gain maximum advantage. No charging defender is a match for them one-to-one, and coaches have nightmares about kick-offs that are run back for touchdowns.

So more and more, at least at the professional level, coaches are demanding that a kickoff specialist be able to boot the ball beyond his opponent's end zone, thus eliminating any possibility for a runback. More and more placekickers seem to be mastering the art of the monster-kick, and sometime in the future the placekick-return specialist may become as obsolete as the drop-kicker.

AFTERWORD

The beautiful feature about kicking is that it represents the ultimate in gridiron democracy. Size and strength are never as important as technique and steel nerve.

At a practical level, the chances for a placekicker or even punter surviving without suffering a crippling injury are enhanced by the lack of physical contact inherent in the kicking game.

And while an older generation of players may find it difficult to adjust to the fact that on a Garo Yepremian's toe or instep hinges the success of their season, more and more players at every level of competition realize now that a good placekicker and a good punter are as vital for victory as a good quarterback.

But perhaps the best assessment of what a kicker contributes to a team's success was voiced a few years back by Weeb Ewbank, the coach for the New York Jets—the Joe Namath Jets.

"Thank God," said Ewbank, a man who is rarely prone to overstatement, "for Jim Turner."